The Mindset Melting Pot

Written and Illustrated by

KJ Walton

Contents

The Value of Growth Mindset :

+   Learning awareness
      Awareness of Learning feelings
      A Learning language

Learning Control & Independence

Fortitude and Banoffee Bee are characters from my first 'Growth Mindset' inspired picture book for children, 'I Can't Do This'. Join them once more in a quest to find out how to create a Growth Mindset culture in the classroom.

Help your pupils set their bubbles free...

Foreword

Having a growth mindset means you live and breathe it in your everyday life — you enjoy finding things challenging (because you know your neurons are firing!), you welcome constructive criticism (because you know it will lead to improvement), you take risks and spread your wings beyond your comfort zone. In Katie's Mindset Melting Pot we have enough information and material to be able to develop our own growth mindsets and to be the best teachers we can be, giving every child we teach their own life-long growth mindset.

I first came across Katie Walton when she sent me a copy of her beautifully self-illustrated and marvellous book 'I Can't Do This', about a character who finally realizes that the answer to learning is that it is journey with future possibilities, along which there are likely to be hold-ups and possible failures. The 'lightbulb' moment for the character, Fortitude, is when he realizes the power of the word 'YET', as in 'I can't do it YET' or 'I don't know YET'. For some time I have recommended this book to teachers as a 'way-in' for helping children understand the emotions attached to the growth mindset.

Since then, Katie's passion has been to apply the findings of Carol Dweck's internationally renowned growth mindset research in her own school, experimenting with practical ways in which teachers can help children develop their own, powerful growth mindsets.

The culmination of her work with children is this wonderful goldmine of growth mindset advice. The book is aimed at 7 to 11 year olds, but most of the activities, and certainly the theory, apply to children of all ages. The book is accessible and teacher-friendly, with a clear route through, from background theory to a host of classroom activities and tasks to practical links with meta-cognition. The detail is important — Katie talks to us in a practical way, with anecdotal evidence and examples of impact, with quotes from children along the way.

Teachers need practical ideas, grounded in real classroom practice, but they also need these to be backed up by research, so the grounding principles are followed rather than the ideas as isolated activities. That is exactly what this book does — links the theory and practice with clarity. Katie's own growth mindset revealed itself when she sent me the first draft of this book and I suggested numerous revisions. People with a fixed mindset might have ignored advice or given up, but Katie forged ahead, just like the characters in her book, despite preparations for her upcoming marriage and the like! The result is a brilliantly polished, developed publication which I will be eagerly promoting in my own work.

Shirley Clarke
April 2015

Acknowledgements

This book has been a labour of love. The ideas inside it have been lived and breathed for some time. My passion for getting it out there and getting it 'just right' could not have been achieved without the help and support of some wonderful people.

My gratitude goes to my parents for their belief and investment in my cause. I thank them too for their editing suggestions and their feedback and criticism! I thank Heather Wadsworth, Keith Wadsworth, Danielle Rowbotham and Scott Rowbotham for performing similar duties with interest and enthusiasm for what I am trying to achieve. Geoffrey Middleton has been a key link in the chain, taking a keen interest in my project and dispatching my books with the greatest of efficiency. I could not do this without him. Similarly, Neil Coleman, who designed and created my website. He has been fantastic to work with and helped to turn my ideas into reality.

I want to take this opportunity to publicly thank the person who sewed the Growth Mindset in me four years ago. Sarah Hinchliffe has been an inspirational role model in my life and her belief in what I could achieve has helped to get me to this point and fostered my own Growth Mindset. I also want to thank the teacher colleagues I have worked with along the way in endeavouring to foster this culture, particularly Catherine Phillips whose enthusiasm has been a delight!

My gratitude also goes to Shirley Clarke for her belief and support for the work I am doing. She is a formidable force in education and her name behind my work is simply amazing. I cannot thank her enough.

Last but by no means least, I want to take this opportunity to thank Damian Middleton, my husband to be, for being my IT support, my sounding board and the voice behind me that pushes me onward because he believes in what I am trying to do. He has had much patience!

You are all an inspiration to me and I am lucky to have you in my life. You are all Growth Mindsetters! Thank you does not really express how grateful I am for your support.

The essence of the Mindset theory from which we begin...

From over three decades of research into motivation, American psychologist Carol Dweck has been working to answer the question:

Why do some people achieve their potential while equally talented others don't?

Her findings have revealed that the answer to this question is not down to ability in itself but whether you regard ability as something that is inherent that must be demonstrated or as something that can be developed.

Through numerous studies, it has been shown how the way you view your brain and intelligence highly affects your motivation in life. Dweck has put together a framework that illustrates two particular ways to view life and learning. The Growth Mindset and the Fixed Mindset. The different Mindsets provide our own internal monologues that go to shape our subsequent behaviour.

Intelligence as a fixed entity V's the incremental nature of learning

The seed of the Fixed Mindset tells us that intelligence is fixed. The brain is seen as a fixed 'entity' and cannot be altered. What we are born with is our lot, so to speak. Conversely, the Growth Mindset tells us that the brain and our intelligence can be developed through effort. The 'incremental' nature of learning is the focus rather than the notion of the brain/intelligence as a 'fixed' entity. Indeed, it has been proven that the more neurons that are fired in the brain when an activity is repeated (practised), the stronger the connections between the synapses become; the learning becomes more embedded.

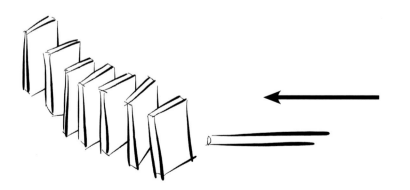

The Mindset domino effect:

Whatever belief you hold about the brain (Fixed or Growth) will lead to different subsequent behaviours. The knock-on effect of these behaviours will ultimately lead to more or less achievement. It dictates whether you will fulfill your potential.

The Fixed Mindset monologue

If you believe that intelligence is fixed and that your brain does not develop, what is particularly damaging is that you are triggering a set of damaging behaviours which will lead to some very detrimental behaviour in terms of learning and being able to reach your full potential. You have a lot to protect in terms of how others view you and your intelligence. Failure is something that will start to define you which you will want to prevent happening at all costs.

- You are less likely to take risks/accept challenges because you might fail

- You don't want others to see you working hard and putting in effort as this means you are not naturally clever

- You do not want to be seen to make mistakes

- If you cannot do something straight away or right first time, you think others will see you as lacking in natural ability

The child feels their intelligence, and in essence their SELF, is being judged as a result of these outcomes.

These ideas will manifest themselves deep within the learning child and without their realisation, will make them behave in ways that will put up barriers to learning new things.

The Growth Mindset monologue

However, there is another way; the Growth Mindset. If you believe intelligence can be developed, this leads to very a very different monologue and subsequent behaviour.

- You see learning as fruitful because it will grow your brain

- You see effort as a positive thing because your brain is working hard

- Failure does not define you; it makes you develop because it is through mistakes that you learn

- You will face challenges, persevere and take risks because you understand these things move you out of your comfort zone and into your learning zone

All of this will help to grow your brain/intelligence. Believing your intellegence can grow is therefore a self fulfilling prophecy.

Taxi driver brains

In support of this, the brains of training taxi drivers have been MRI scanned and the Hippocampi of these individuals (responsible for long term memory and spatial navigation) have visibly enlarged. It has been shown that, after studying for a series of gruelling exams of 25,000 streets within a radius of 10km of Charing Cross Station over three to four years, the trainees brains change and grow. The size of the memory centres for these people are significantly above average. The studies carried out show that it is the training that causes the growth. Evidence has shown that the brain can grow and develop. Neuroscientist Howard Eichenbaum at Boston University has said,

'It shows you can produce profound changes within the brain through training. That's a big deal.'

Seeing the point of learning

The Mindset that individuals choose to adopt will highly influence the way they behave, particularly in relation to motivation. An individual does not necessarily possess one Mindset or the other; one might display evidence of both at different times. However, the beauty of this theory is that Mindsets can be altered (whenever they occur), simply by understanding the theory and by echoing it's messages though language and behaviour. Through our awareness of the theory, we are in a position to change. It's a case of,

'I can't do this YET'/ 'I don't know YET' (FUTURE) not, 'I can't do this '/ 'I don't know.' (NOW)

The latter is not the end of the story. The addition of the word YET allows for a consideration of the future and potential. Without YET, a child's difficulty is stuck in the here and now and they are more likely to give in to the negative feelings that being stuck can bring with it and give up. Having this awareness is a powerful position in which to be. It gives the individual choice of where they want to go in life and learning. It can dramatically change an individual's motivation to work for something. In regards to children, the motivation to learn becomes significantly more inviting; learning has a significant value and point. **YET** is a powerful and significant little word; it means so much in relation to learning.

Enabling self-regulation

In being exposed to the Mindset theory and its ideas, children are enabled to make their own informed choices about learning; they are able to become independent learners and that makes for a vibrant, exciting classroom, full of purpose and learning talk.

Children are more able to self-regulate and this avoids learned helplessness.

Where they are NOW is not the end result; they can change where they are now through effort. They need to understand;

- What the Mindsets are

- Why it is important to develop the Growth Mindset as opposed to the Fixed Mindset

- How they can change their habits to help themselves develop the Growth Mindset and subsequently their learning

You cannot improve achievement unless your pupils have the right learning attitude in place. A Mindset culture in the classroom is what is needed in order for children to reach their potential and achieve more.

(To learn more about the specifics of Dweck's research, see 'Mindsets: The Theory of Success' by Professor Carol Dweck).

The Holy Grail?

There is one last important point to make here. The Growth Mindset alone will not lead to high achievement.

There must be a consideration of powerful learning methods and strategies that build from the vital foundations that possessing a Growth Mindset provides.

There are other texts that will highlight these practices in detail, for example, '**Outstanding Formative Assessment**' by Shirley Clarke. 'The Mindset Melting Pot' offers ideas that can be used to create the right learning culture in the classroom from which to bounce. Without this, the other 'stuff' can prove fruitless.

You need to instil a 'learning attitude' in children to allow learning to happen. Teaching children about Growh Mindset will enable them to switch on their learning muscles to ensure success and achievement. Children with a want and thirst to learn is at the forefront of successful education. This is what a Growth Mindset will give them. Confidence and self esteem will also be raised as a knock-on effect.

One task before you start...

Look at the grid on the following page. If you were to pick some ideas that often "fit" you, which would they be?

Obviously it depends on the context but if you were to choose them generally, which would you go for? In beginning the Mindset journey with children, it is important that adults working with the theory get to understand it and unpick it themselves. Where are you in terms of your Mindset? It helps to understand the theory and if you are working on your Mindset as well as the children and sharing that experience with them, they will see you in a new way that will build a wonderful atmosphere of trust in the classroom. I have seen this in action; it really encourages children to take risks in their learning. You are all embarking on the learning journey together. They are not alone. It is an amazing journey worth having on a personal level. If you can do this, you will be more successful nurturing this culture in your classroom.

Find your own Growth Mindset

Teachers are powerful role models. We must never underestimate the influence that we have over the children we teach. Therefore, if we are expecting children to adopt a Growth Mindset, we must find our own. This project is the result of me finding my own Growth Mindset!

The children will become more confident and ideally more passionate about what they are trying to achieve in the classroom. Commitment to the cause is essential if you are going to make a real difference. I hope the ideas in this book will help you to develop that passion. If you stick with the exploration, you will see a difference in the way children talk and behave. If you are keen, they will be too and will start to talk the talk without you needing to push too much. I have embarked on this journey with four classes and each have reacted with interest to Mindset because it became a regular diet in the classroom. Once you start to see and hear the children's responses to Mindset, you will be hooked!

Start thinking about your own Mindset... Be as honest with yourself as you can! You will get more out of this process if you are.

Use the statements from the grid on the following page. These statements are either Fixed or Growth Mindset linked. Which Mindset each statement falls into is detailed on page 19. Try not to look at these definitions until you have thought about which of the statements 'best fit' you. Make a list of these.

I like challenges.	If something is tricky, sometimes I give up.	I know that putting in effort is important.	It doesn't matter if I fail.	I work hard because it helps me.
I know my own limits.	I don't know what my talents are yet but I am willing to work hard to find out.	Putting in effort makes me smart and talented.	I like being praised for my hard work.	I don't like getting things wrong.
I am willing to develop my learning.	I feel uncomfortable if I don't know how to do something.	I'm not that clever.	I don't mind asking for help after I have tried by myself.	If I find something hard, I practise it.
I like my work to be praised.	I am willing to change.	I have lots of talents but I don't know what they all are yet.	I feel intelligent when I get everything right.	I worry about what others think of me.
I'm afraid of not being good at something.	I'm not worried about what other people think of me.	I don't like people to criticise my learning.	Putting in effort shows other people that I'm not smart.	I work hard because it makes other people happy.

Growth Mindset Labels

Growth Mindset	Fixed Mindset
I like challenges.	If something is tricky, sometimes I give up.
I know that putting in effort is important.	I know my own limits.
It doesn't matter if I fail.	If I get something wrong I don't try again.
I work hard because it helps me.	I don't like getting things wrong.
I don't know what my talents are yet but I'm willing to work hard to find out.	I feel uncomfortable if I don't know how to do something.
I like being praised for my hard work.	I'm not that clever.
Putting in effort makes me smart and talented.	I like my work to be praised.
I don't mind asking for help after I have tried by myself.	I feel intelligent when I get everything right.
If I find something hard, I practise it.	I worry about what others think of me.
I am willing to develop my learning.	I'm afraid about not being good at something.
I have lots of talents but I don't know what they all are yet.	I don't like people criticising my learning/work.
I'm not worried about what other people think of me.	Putting in effort shows other people I'm not smart.
	I work hard because it makes other people happy.

To begin at the beginning...

Solving two learning problems with one bit of theory.

When I first read Carol Dweck's book, 'Mindset' 3 years ago, it was because the Head Teacher of the School I was working in knew something about the theory. She thought it could be something that would make an impact on the children at our school, many of whom were bright but were, as we discovered, particularly 'Fixed' in their Mindsets.

It was apparent that there was something that was not quite right as these bright children, who were being given both creative and challenging material to learn with, were often heard to say; "**This is easy.**" What didn't fit with this assertion was the amount of effort they were putting in which was not particularly staggering for children who were seemingly 'above average' and the standard was not always as good as we might have expected from these children. They were not extending the work in the challenging ways that were possible. They were doing the minimum to achieve what they needed to but not pushing themselves further. The behaviour displayed was limiting these children which was frustrating as they had ability but also an attitude that prevented any significant learning that would move them on:

- They were firmly rooted in their comfort zone

- They did not want to 'lose face' in front of their peers

At the same time, there were other children who would find the learning challenging. Rather than accepting the challenges as such, they would regularly give up. In one particular class I taught, there was a boy who found writing very tricky. Almost every other sentence that came out of his mouth at the beginning of the year was negative and defeatist; "I can't do this"; "It's too hard,"; "What's the point?"; "I can't be bothered!"; "I don't care!" Ironically, I believed he did care. If he didn't, why would he make these feelings so apparent to all around him? I was concerned on two levels;

- With this kind of attitude, how would he make progress and learn anything of significance, now and in the future? (He would end up hating learning because he didn't understand the value of challenges and that everybody found learning tricky at times- he seemed to think he was alone in his feelings.)

- What effect was he having on those around him? I could already see that his attitude was starting to spread around the class like a Mexican Wave (but a lot less fun for those both involved and observing from the outside!)

We had two very different but equally damaging attitudes at play in the school. The question was, 'What can we do to challenge both of these issues?' My Head Teacher always used to say at staff meetings, "This is not a problem, it is a challenge for which we need to find a solution." A very Growth Mindset attitude (I realised later) but one which was particularly relevant in the process we were about to go through as a school. As it turned out, the solution to our problems was Mindset. By embarking on the Mindset journey, we were able to kill two birds with one stone or solve two problems with one bit of theory!

Recognising Mindset moments

For a school to embark on the Mindset journey, the individual teacher needs to think carefully about Mindset theory and fully embrace it. Once the understanding is in place, strengthened through exploration within the classroom, **the culture can be developed within the school when everybody is on board.** Obviously to be successful in developing it as a school culture, it is important for all staff to go through this process. They all need to recognise their own Mindset moments and be willing to consider them.

Why is the Growth Mindset culture the key to unlocking powerful learning? I think I became so passionate about this topic for three main reasons;

1. After reading the book, it sat in my mind and I realised that I was having more Fixed Mindset moments than I ever would have imagined. This is probably true of most of us. Without realising it, many of us are controlled by a Fixed Mindset voice in our heads that stops us grasping opportunities and reaching our full potential. The power of the theory is not that it is rocket science but that it gives us awareness. Once we have awareness, that is the start of altering our behaviour; it is the same for children which is why teaching it explicitly is so important.

2. It motivates children to work hard because they **see a point to learning.**

3. It works. Maybe more overtly for some children than others but it works. What happened to the boy I mentioned above after a year of Mindset training? Below is the comment he made on his report slip at the end of the year about his achievements over the year. With no prompting from me, he wrote:

Growth Mindset helped me so much this year at the start of the year I always said stuff like, "im rubbish!" "I can't do this!" But now I haven't said it for ages. This is because of growth mindset.

Having known what this boy had been like in terms of his attitude to learning at the beginning of the year, I was thrilled when he handed me this bit of paper. He was a much happier child by the end of the year and I would go so far as to suggest that he actually enjoyed being in the classroom. From that moment, I was hooked on spreading the 'Growth Mindset' word and coming up with the ways and means by which to get children involved with the theory. It is a project that is continually growing and evolving.

I Can't Do This!

I published my first children's picture book, 'I Can't Do This'' last year to open the Mindset discussion with children in the classroom; this was the start of my Mindset journey. I have been overwhelmed with the response and demand for it. In talking to other teachers from all over the country, I know that people are wanting to embark on the Mindset journey in schools. I am continually being asked; how did you do it in the classroom? '**The Mindset Melting Pot**' is the response to that question. There are lots of bits and pieces I have done over the three years I have been exploring Mindset, some that have worked better than others. What I have included here are the ideas that have worked well. I have worked with Key Stage 2 children (age 7-11) in the main and therefore, this is where these activities are based. However, that is not to say that these ideas could not be used or adapted for children of a younger age.

Tried and tested ideas

I am excited by this theory and have therefore enjoyed exploring with children how it can evolve into a school culture. I'm sure there are a lot more developments to come but I believe this is certainly a good start. What I hope you will find useful and reassuring is that I am a working teacher. These ideas are tried and tested. I have watched children get equally excited by the theory as they develop their understanding of it. Children have been grateful to have the theory revealed to them and have told me how it has helped to motivate and grow them in their learning.

Nurturing independent learners

It has enabled them to take control of their learning and become much more **independent**. I have seen low self esteem issues lessen and confidence grow. If I had not seen all of this, believe me, I would not be endeavouring to spread the word. I am a teacher – I have little time for anything else!

If you like the sound of all this, do read on...

How to use the book

When pulling together all the 'bits and pieces' I have done in relation to Mindset, I realised that they fell into some distinct areas;

1. **Beginnings (starting points).**
2. **Activities to Explore Mindset with children.**
3. **Behaviours to adopt in the classroom.**
4. **Supportive Aids to have displayed and refer to in the classroom.**

The '**Beginnings**' and '**Activities**' are needed to begin **exploring what the two different Mindsets are** and why we want to have the Growth Mindset as much as possible in life. The 'Beginnings' section also considers some forms of qualitative measure of the effects that the Mindset culture may have on your pupils.

The '**Behaviours**' and '**Supportive Aids**' sections are then vital in order to **build and sustain the culture** that then keeps the messages and ideas of Mindset alive in the classroom throughout the year.

The book is separated into these parts, the start of each section beginning with a mind map showing the areas covered within it.

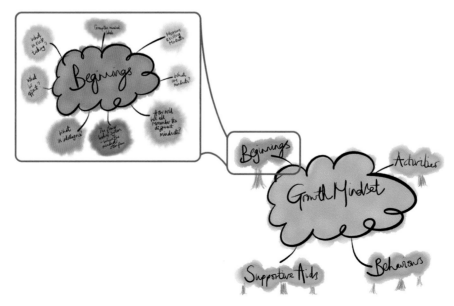

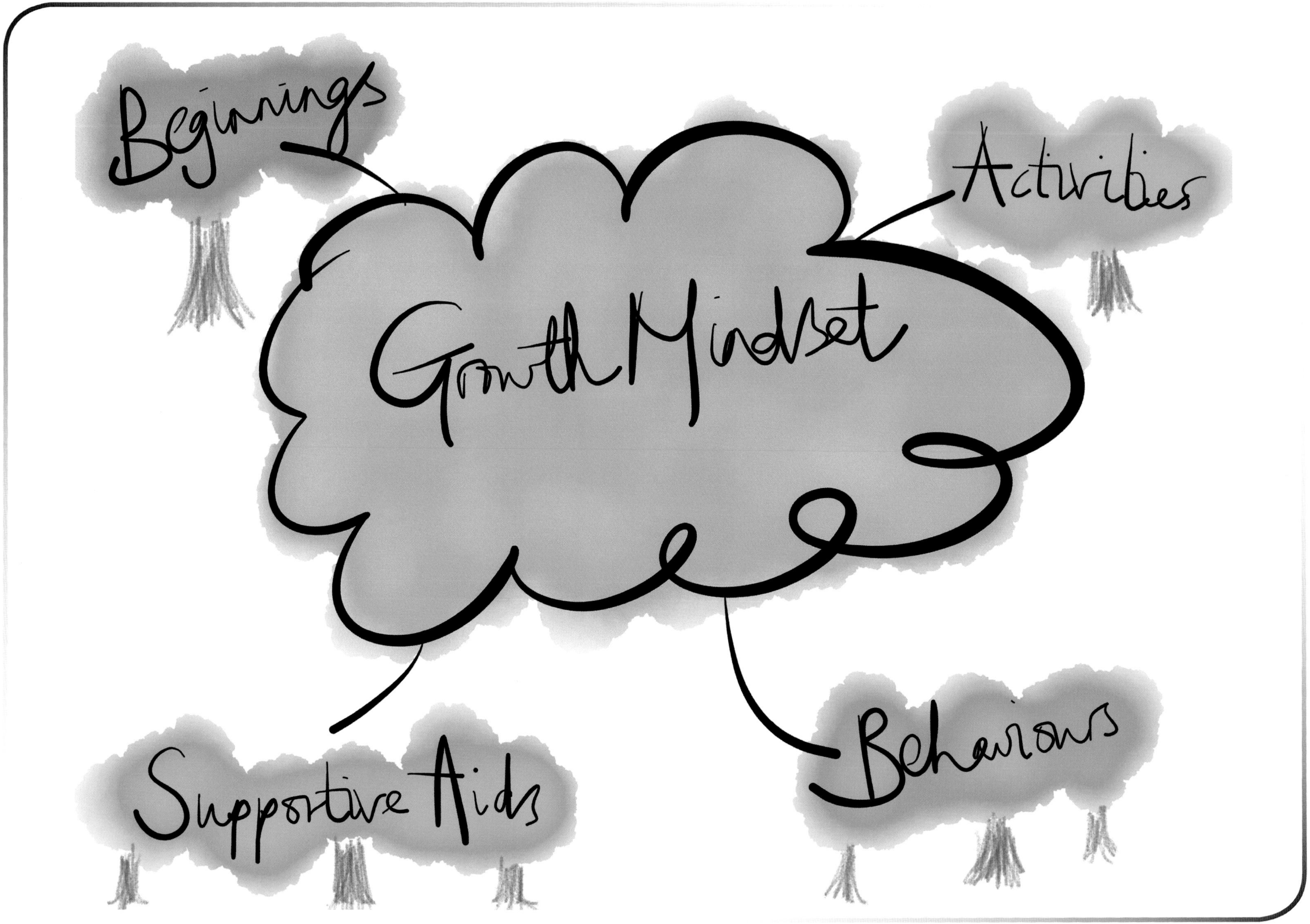

Growth Mindset

- Behaviors
- Supportive Aids
- Activities
- Beginnings

Beginnings

What is risk taking?

Group the mindset labels

Measure existing Mindsets

What is effort?

What are mindsets?

What is intelligence?

The flower belief system — where the mindsets stem from

How will we all remember the different mindsets?

Something that is worth doing, if you have not yet done anything with the children about Mindset, is to measure the effect that it has once you do start to work with the ideas.

The following exercise not only allows you to do this (as it can be done before the process begins and after as a measure of change) but it also starts to open up the discussion of many aspects of the Mindset theory. The pupils should complete the following task independently and not talk to others whilst doing it as you do not want them to influence each other's thoughts. Tell them to be as thoughtful and honest as they can be. There are no right or wrong answers. Explain that their honesty is much more valuable.

Print off the outline of a body which is to represent them as a person (the high resolution image is also available to download from my website - **www.growthmindset.org**).

Give each of the children the labels that are printed on page 18. They should read through the labels carefully (support given to those that need it) and cut out the labels that they think apply to them. They should then stick these around the body. This will give you an idea as to where the children are in their thinking about themselves. Some labels are more Fixed Mindset orientated and others more Growth Mindset orientated (see **page 19** for a listing of the phrases and which Mindset each phrase is linked to). The children may well have a mixture of the two as people tend not to be Fixed or Growth Mindset in entirety but show elements of both.

The important bit, eventually, is to start recognising when they are having Fixed Mindset moments so that the behaviour can be altered. I found this exercise very interesting. It highlighted attitudes of some children that I never would have expected. Some low self esteem issues that you never realised were there can be exposed which can alter the way you deal with some children.

Children measure their own Mindsets

After a good period of time learning about Growth Mindset's ideals and endeavouring to live life by them, this exercise can be done again for example at the end of the year. **Ask them what differences they can see in themselves from the two versions (before and after) and discuss their findings. Find out how their Mindsets have changed.** It is a great exercise for them to do as this **increases their awareness of how their attitudes are a big part of learning.** It shows them that they are ultimately in control of how they choose to behave in relation to their learning, nobody else. **It also shows them that they have the power to change things that are not helping them to progress.** This is a powerful realisation and holds much greater weight than if the teacher had said it to them. They can see it for themselves; this is all part of the process in becoming a more independent learner.

So what Mindset am I?

An essential starting point

The following activity not only encourages them to explore ideas and thinking that create the different Mindsets but without realising, they will start to define it by themselves. This makes their understanding of what the Mindsets are more influential as they feel they have been a part of the creation of the definition. This helps them to own it.

Print off the Growth and Fixed Mindset labels on the following page individually onto A4 paper and laminate them. Decide how you will group the children to do this activity, I suggest 5 or 6 children in each. You will need as many of these sets of laminates as you have groups (for example, table groups). You will be able to re-use these and one set will be used to make a display at the end of the activity. (If you are creating a school wide culture, all classes could borrow the sets at different times). **When you give the sets to the groups, ensure that they are all mixed up and not grouped as Fixed and Growth Mindset thoughts.**

The thoughts are both Fixed and Growth Mindset orientated but the children do not know this; indeed **at this stage they do not even know what Mindsets are.**

One instruction is given; **"I want you to sort these ideas out into groups."**

That is it. You do not tell them how many groups, you do not tell them what sort of groups you are after. The children should read through the labels/phrases to see what is there and have a discussion about how they could be grouped. The activity encourages them to process what the ideas are and what they could possibly mean. Some may obviously go together, some not so obviously. They must decide and agree as a group.

Question: "If you were to name the groups you have created, what would you name them and why?"

Fixed Mindset

You avoid Challenges
You give up easily
You see effort as pointless
You ignore useful or negative feedback
You hate criticism
You hate making mistakes
You feel threatened by the success of others
Achieve less than full potential
Deterministic view of the world - it is how it is and cannot be changed

Growth Mindset

You believe intelligence can be developed - leads to a desire to learn
You embrace challenges
You persist in the face of set-backs
Set-backs don't discourage you
You see set-backs as an opportunity to learn (not worried about looking good)
You see effort as the path to mastery
Learn from criticism
Learn from mistakes
Find lessons and inspiration in the success of others
Reach higher levels of achievement
Greater sense of free will (being able to achieve what you want)

Students define the Mindsets themselves

When I ran this activity with a new class, all the groups came up with different ideas of what the groups could be called but the labels were essentially grouped in the same way. This, in itself, starts to define what Mindset is all about, as the children think about what to title the groups.

Having discussed the different ideas together and looked at how all groups had physically grouped labels, I then discussed the idea of individuals possessing a Fixed and Growth Mindset and positioned these labels in the correct groups. You will probably find they have created these groupings themselves, without knowing what the Mindsets are. If there are any differences, this makes for an interesting discussion point when you are explaining which thoughts fall into which Mindset.

The grouped labels form an immediate display that goes on the wall. It is a display that means something important to the pupils as they have deeply considered the ideas and processed them. In essence, they have created the display together and defined the different Mindsets themselves. The display should be referred to throughout the year during day to day lessons to keep the messages alive and thought about in practice. This is important as it establishes HOW the ideas are a reality in their learning. The thoughts are given life and meaning to their own learning context.

There is a lot more to do in terms of their understanding of what the Mindsets are at this point but this is a good place to start. It is also a handy reference point when you all refer back to the ideas throughout the year. If you want to measure the children's own Mindsets, you need to ensure you have done the previous activity before you do the this activity or the children's responses may well be influenced.

What are Mindsets?

Accessibility

The Mindset theory that Dweck presents to us is exactly that; theory. It offers great ideas but somehow we have to package it in a way that is accessible to children and make it possible to work with day to day.

There are documents that can be found on the internet when you Google 'Mindset' to help define the terms in a more concise way than the theory that Dweck gives us but when I came to work these ideas with children, I still felt that they were not particularly memorable for them. I therefore worked on constructing a framework that I felt the children I was teaching would be able to grasp more easily. The labels on the following page are what I came up with.

Memorise

There are still several labels to remember but I have paired a Fixed Mindset label with an opposing Growth Mindset one to make them easier for children to remember. There are still, in total, 24 labels (which is a lot).

Recall

However, once the idea of the label is recalled for either the Growth or Fixed Mindset, it is easy to recall the opposite label it is paired with. Therefore, there are only 12 labels for the children to learn and I have come up with some fun games for the children to play in order to do this. Once they start referring to these on a regular basis, they will become embedded in their minds. It may seem a lot for children to learn but trust me when I say they will learn them – children often surprise us with what they can do! We need to stretch them. Let them show you what they can do. Besides, there are always those who catch on more quickly and they will start to bring others with them over time. The more and more you refer to the labels in class during learning activities, the more embedded and recalled they will become. You should also get them to start applying them as the ideas start to embed.

The Mindset labels to be learned and referred to by everyone in the classroom are given on the following page:

Fixed Mindset	Growth Mindset
Avoid challenges.	Love challenges.
The world is fixed.	The world can change.
Ignore feedback.	Use feedback.
Hate criticism.	Learn from criticism.
Hate making mistakes.	Learn from mistakes.
Threatened by others success.	Inspired by others success.
Intelligence stays the same.	Intelligence can develop.
Give up easily.	Keep going.
Effort is pointless.	Effort is important.
See setbacks as failure.	Learn from setbacks.
Putting in effort shows you're not smart.	Putting in effort makes you smart.
Achieve less.	Achieve more.

How will we remember the different Mindsets?

Embedding Mindset ideals

The table of Mindset labels is an important resource in the beginnings of Mindset. Later on, as the labels become more and more embedded, it will be less and less important to have these physically available as the children will be able to recall them. I have them displayed on my classroom wall so they can be regularly referred to. It is quite fun to have the occasional test/quiz to see which ones children can remember. I have adapted a few simple games/activities to get the children to **memorise the labels** as follows:

Kim's Game

This is an adaptation of the old party game classic of removing an item from a tray and having to work out which item is missing. Get the children into pairs or threes, each group with a table of labels for both Mindsets. Get them to cut out the labels together and then lay them out on a table in front of them. They should take a few minutes to read through and possibly discuss them in order to memorise them. It is best for them to do this with the labels laid out in their groups with the opposite Mindset label next to it. Then, one child turns away from the labels whilst the other removes one (or possibly even a pair) and mixes the remaining labels up on the table, still face up. The aim of the game is for the partner to turn back and find which one (or pair) is missing. Resourceful children will spot that by pairing them up, they will find the missing label more easily!

Indian Tepee (original drama game)

This game is one I adapted from a drama game that I played when I was young. The story is told that a long time ago, in Native America, when an Indian child was born, the Indian Chief would emerge from the Tepee where the birth had taken place and look around him. The first thing that he saw would become the name of the child. For instance, it might be 'Raging River' or 'Blue Mountain'. The drama game that then came from this tale was that children were instructed to invent their own Indian name in a similar way, by looking around them. The children would sit in a circle and one by one they would share the name that they had created and share a simple gesture that would illustrate it. The other children would repeat the name and the gesture. The idea was to try and remember other people's names and gestures so that the following game could be played: A child would begin by saying their Indian name and repeating the gesture. This would be followed by them making the letter 'T' with their fingers whilst saying the word 'to' and then following this with another child's Indian name and gesture. The process would then be repeated and thus the names would be past randomly around the circle. **The game encourages memorisation by linking action to words.**

Mindset Version

The Mindset version of this game is for children to **use the different label phrases** (both Fixed and Growth) instead of looking around them to invent a name. They should choose a label phrase and invent their own gesture to go with it. The phrase and the gesture is then passed around the circle in the same way as described above. The game works best in groups of about fifteen so if you have a class of thirty it might work better to split them in half and have two games being played simultaneously. The game can last as long as you want but it is good to try and get all the children's labels and gestures picked so that they all have a turn. The children could be told the aim of the game is to have all the children picked at least once. The repetition of phrases and children finding ways to remember them is part of the **memorising and embedding process.** An extension to the game is to simply pass the gestures around the circle without words being spoken. This could make for a calm session!

Get the Mindset definitions memorised and embedded in everyone's minds.

Mindset Football

You want as many ways as possible to repeat and embed the Mindset phrases so that you can then refer to them and start unpicking what they mean in practical, classroom situations.

The goal of this football game is to score as many Mindset goals as possible. Split the class into two teams, one is the Fixed Mindset team and the other Growth Mindset. All the children walk freely around a pitch (open space) and when they meet a member of the opposite team they shake hands to initiate a tackle. They could define themselves as a team in some way, eg one team takes off their jumpers and the other leaves their jumpers on. The Growth Mindset team member says a Growth Mindset phrase and the Fixed Mindset team member responds with the opposite Growth Mindset phrase (or vice versa). They then move on and tackle another person with a different phrase from their team's Mindset phrase bank and repeat the process. They do this as many times as they can in the given time. Encourage them to try and use different phrases each time they tackle an opponent.

After a set period of time on this, for example two or three minutes, call for half time. The teams come together and together write down as many of the opposing team's phrases that they have heard (or not) as they can. These should be shared with the referee (teacher) who writes them down in a goal on the board. Any that are missed could be recorded on the outside of the goal with a special effort made to try and remember these ones. This should be repeated with the other team in a different goal. There may be a winning team here but hopefully a draw. The best result would be a draw of '12 All' as then the teams have collectively remembered all the phrases for the Mindset they are trying to recall!

They then swap Mindsets so the Fixed team become Growth and vice versa. The second half is then played and the task repeated so that all the children have a go at remembering the phrases from each Mindset.

The flower belief system

I came up with the diagrams following on pages 37 and 38, to illustrate to children why the **different seeds of the two Mindsets** lead to such different ideas and behaviours about learning. I think it is also a useful visual representation for adults as well. It is a quick and simple method of illustrating why the seeds (underlying beliefs about the brain and intelligence) can lead to such different behaviours in relation to learning.

I felt it was necessary for children to have some sort of understanding of this. Obviously, children are not going to understand Dweck's theory in the same detail as adults but I wanted to provide children with something that would show them why being aware of the different Mindsets is valuable. They need to realise its power and importance to want to work with the ideas. Some children may understand it better than others but it is important to at least give them the opportunity to make the links between it and their own behaviour. It is a link in the chain that goes to help them become more independent learners and give them a reason for displaying certain behaviours as they can see why it reinforces the different Mindset seeds. It goes some way to explaining why choosing a certain way to behave re-feeds the seed at the bottom of the diagram (whether that be Fixed or Growth); whatever seed you follow becomes a **self fulfilling prophecy** as the arrow on each diagram shows.

Some discussion around this flower and what it means to them would be useful and powerful. The following questions could be asked as part of this discussion;

1. **Why do you think a flower has been used to represent these ideas?**
2. **Can you think of a different drawing / metaphor you could use to represent the ideas? Why would this work? This could be discussed and developed in groups.**

These questions require deep thinking and may be more suitable for older pupils (Year 5/6). However, I do not think the questions should be avoided with younger pupils as often the creative insights these children offer are extremely valuable. Many children enjoy the kind of stretching and thinking that these kinds of questions allow. I have been amazed and astounded by the ideas that Mindset has pulled from children that I would never have expected. It might be that you get some good ideas and thinking from this. However, if the children you are working with find it too challenging at this stage, then move on. It might be something that they will work with more easily when they have more understanding of Mindset and have worked with the principles for longer. It could be an activity to come back to at a later date.

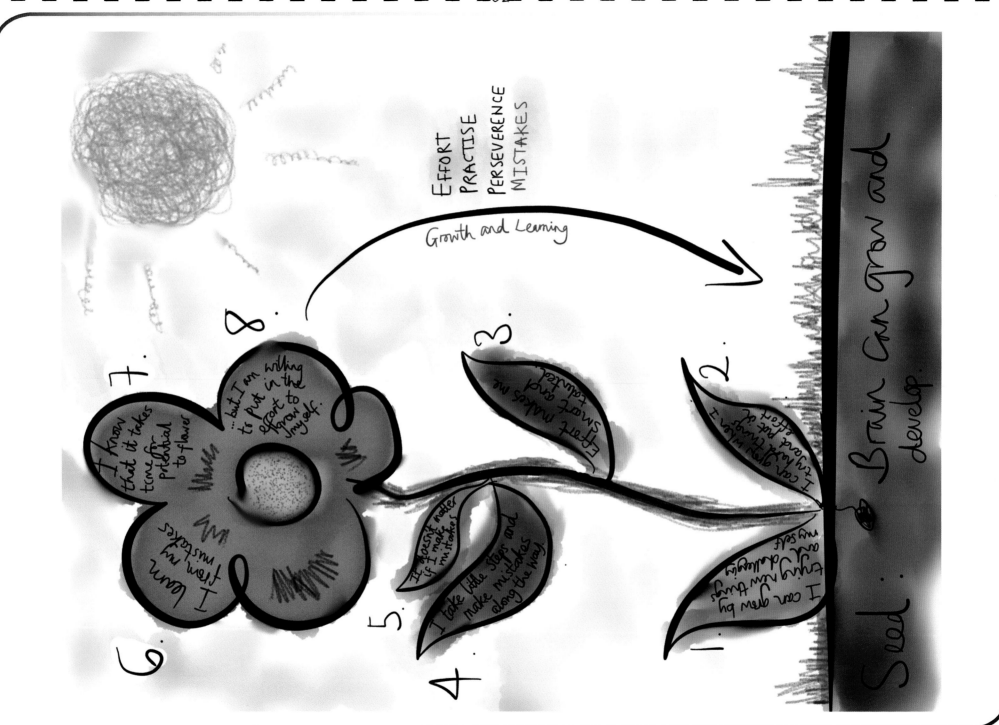

What is intelligence?

The questions below could be reproduced and given to children to consider a definition of intelligence. As adults, we have our own notions about intelligence but it is a concept that is rarely talked about with young children. Considering children are tested in terms of their intelligence against the National Curriculum, this is surprising and I believe dangerous. We may not outwardly talk about testing as a measure of intelligence but for children who go through this experience of being measured against their peers at an early age, this must certainly be an assumption that they reach without any input having been given.

Children will create their own definition of intelligence based on comparing themselves to peers which is what the testing promotes. These ideas need challenging so that children are not 'put off' learning because they think they are not 'intelligent'. Encourage children to consider and challenge their ideas by asking them questions;

- What is intelligence?
- Is there a definition of intelligence that everybody agrees on?
- Are you born intelligent or can you develop it?
- What does intelligence look like?
- What does intelligence sound like?
- Is everybody intelligent?
- Can a test result show how intelligent an individual is?
- Are there different kinds of intelligence?
- Who do you know who you think is intelligent – why?
- Who of our Mindset celebrities are intelligent and why?
- Were these people born intelligent?
- What evidence do they have that these people are intelligent?
- What have they achieved? How did they achieve it?
- This could be linked back to 'Mindset Quotes' – who do the children know who might follow these mantras?

Children's ideas about intelligence

The starting point of the Mindset theory is that either intelligence is fixed, what you are born with is what you have and this you cannot change, or your brain/intelligence can develop and grow each time you fire those neurons to push yourself out of your comfort zone. In pushing children towards the scientific truth of the latter, we need to understand their preconceived ideas about the definition of intelligence and challenge the idea that you are born with intelligence.

The danger of the 'intelligence' label

In considering 'Intelligence' against the Mindset backdrop, there are several reasons why an unpicking of intelligence is important.

For individuals with Fixed Mindset tendencies, the need to protect how intelligent you are perceived to be is extremely high. If you only have a certain amount of intelligence (as the Fixed Mindset believes) you will do everything you can to show you have a lot.

A test score is not the destination, merely an event in the journey

Many children are so focused on getting a top score or beating their peers that they will do whatever it takes to achieve this. For these children, their intelligence is defined by top end results and they will do whatever they need to do in order to get those results. In her studies, Dweck found this obsession with achieving the perfect end result could lead children to cheat or lie about their achievements. This does nothing to develop intelligence. Without intervention, this is the behaviour that testing encourages. **Children need to understand that test results do not define them and a result merely reflects where they are now, not where they could be in the future.** They also need to understand that effort is the key to getting good results. The danger is that, without intervention from adults, a test result for children could obscure the word YET and instead highlight the NOW as a definitive full stop.

Challenge children's definitions of intelligence

There are ideas that children hold about intelligence that the Growth Mindset theory will challenge. Just as teachers need to uncover previous understanding in children's ideas before teaching subjects, so too it is useful to understand what children believe about intelligence when embarking on the Growth Mindset journey.

Do not be afraid to have this discussion. Hold in your mind that the **main ideas** you want to guide pupils through are:

- People are not born intelligent; intelligence happens through effort, perseverance and learning from mistakes, having set-backs, listening to feedback etc. (all the Growth Mindset 'stuff').

- Intelligence can come in many forms.

- The idea that an individual is 'intelligent' comes across as finite; we are never the complete article; there is always more to learn.

- If you perceive yourself to be intelligent, you may well stop yourself from developing because you see yourself as the complete article. This may cause you to stay in your comfort zone and avoid challenges as you want to 'protect' your **intelligent** status; you do not want to be seen to put in effort or make mistakes.

- Defining intelligence is tricky and people hold different views about it; this illustrates why we must be careful about how we use this term. It can hold a lot of weight when actually it is a term that has instigated much debate, both now and in the past. It is a term which has powerful connotations that cloud beliefs we have about ourselves. This could be enough to stop us from doing things if we deem ourselves unintelligent. This is life changing. It could prevent people from fulfilling their potential.

For adults this is a danger to be considered and acted upon; for children this is a catastrophe that could be diverted.

How to tackle 'intelligence' with children:

- Ask the children to think about and answer the questions on page 39.

- Using these ideas, have a discussion with children about what they think intelligence is and how you become intelligent.

- Challenge ideas by asking questions about them; force children to challenge their current thinking about these ideas.

When discussing test results in this discussion, challenge the idea that a test score shows how intelligent you are at something. It is merely a stepping stone. It can help us clarify where we need to go next in our learning. (For those children who find tests daunting, this is a reassuring thought.) A delightful animation produced by Peter Reynolds that explores this idea can be found on YouTube.com by searching under, 'The Testing Camera'.

It is good for children to explore 'intelligence' in order to realise it is not as easy to define as they might first think. They will most likely want to tell you that intelligence is how clever someone is– but what does 'being clever' mean and are you just born clever? Individuals will agree and disagree about certain ideas and so they should, as adults do. **There are no easy answers and to define themselves and others using this label is tricky. The main idea that children should appreciate from a Growth Mindset perspective is that intelligence does not just happen. It is developed, cultivated and worked for.**

It could well be agreed, at the end of this discussion, that we are all intelligent in different ways. The children's book, '**All Kinds of Ways to Be Smart**' by Judy Lalli reflects this idea. Your Mindset celebrities will also illustrate this idea.

We need to end a culture of children being afraid to learn because they're too busy covering up their difficulties and proving how much intelligence they have. They need to consider what intelligence is and realise it is a dangerous way to define themselves and others. They need to understand that everybody is 'a work in progress' and not the finished article.

What is effort?

In the same way that children need to consider a definition of intelligence, they also need to consider their understanding of effort. **How do we know if effort is being displayed?** This is something that should be referred to on a regular basis and therefore, children should be clear what is meant by effort. Dictionary definitions are a good way in to such a discussion but what ideas and anecdotes can children add to this? It is important that a shared notion be reached. Your own phrases and words should be documented and displayed for the children to refer to. The more input the children have in this process, the more they will own it and the more it will mean to them. As with a discussion on intelligence, questions about effort could form part of a school interactive display inviting children to respond to the following questions:

- **What is effort?**
- **How do we know that effort is happening?**
- **How can you ensure you put effort into your learning?**

A set of post-it notes could be left for children on which to write their ideas. The ideas could be collated (maybe by the Mindset Committee) and this is something that could then be shared in an assembly in order to come up with a school-wide definition of **Effort.**

Another way to get children thinking about this and also involving families might be to set the following challenge as a school wide project:

'What is effort?' Explore this idea as creatively as you can.

Effort rating

In many schools, there is some sort of self assessment system in place whereby at the end of a lesson, children rate where they are in their understanding of a concept and write it next to the Learning Objective of the lesson. In a similar way, children could be asked to think about where they would rate the amount of effort they put into a lesson. I am not suggesting that this should be shared as they would probably not be willing to share if they felt they had not put in a good amount of effort but as a rhetorical question at the end of a lesson, it might be useful to get them to **consider if they were working with effort** (easier now with a shared definition). **If not, why might that be and how could they ensure more effort was put into their learning in future? A visual on the wall suggesting effort levels could work well for a lot of children.**

Define it

What is risk taking?

Having a Growth Mindset is largely about **taking risks** to draw you out of your comfort zone and into challenges that are new to you in order to grow and progress. Therefore, I think a discussion with children about **what they think risk taking is** and **what it looks like** is important. You need to agree how you are going to record when this behaviour is happening in the classroom. In this way, they will be aware of it happening around them, even if it is not them that is displaying it at a given moment. It might even encourage a bit of competition for some positive behaviour! The children will reinforce the message to each other but the adults around must acknowledge and be pleased about the behaviour being displayed in order to reinforce it.

Celebrate the occurrence of risk-taking in learning

Make a class list with the children's ideas which can be displayed. You could even put up a display inviting children to tell you what they think risk taking is on post-its: another interactive school display (it could be part of the intelligence one). Some sort of chart could then be put together in classes so that when these moments happen, it could be recorded. For example, on a star with the child's name on it or a chart with each child's name and spaces for stars next to their name. Another idea might be to have a jar with buttons added to it when such a behaviour is shown. It is then a group effort to fill the jar. There could be some sort of group reward at the point at which the jar is filled. I like this idea the best as it shows 'we are all on this risk taking journey together.' It is also a behaviour that could contribute to '**Mindset Twitter**™', see page 46. It also links well to the '**Learning Buttons**' which I will consider later.
N.B: When considering risk-taking, make sure that you link this idea to learning (we don't want any accidents!)

A deeper exploration

Children could design a piece of artwork entitled '**Risk Taking**'. This could take the form of a 3D model or a piece of 2D art on a piece of paper. This kind of exercise allows them the creative space to consider what risk taking is more deeply. It could form part of a project/competition across the school. I love seeing the creative ideas children come up with in relation to such ideas; they often think of extremely thoughtful creations that adults would have great difficulty in coming up with! It also encourages the discussion of these ideas at home.

Mindset journal

Mindset Twitter™

Recording thoughts about Mindset

One of the early Mindset activities I tried out was the keeping of a Mindset Journal. At the start of the Year, I asked all the children to bring in their own little notepad that could be used for this purpose. For any that could not bring one, I would provide them with one. Children love bringing their own stationery to school so most children did this willingly.

The idea was to give the children a set moment every day to fill in any Growth or Fixed Mindset moments into their journal; they were asked to record what happened and what their response was or could have been on reflection. This has worked better with some classes than others but it is quite difficult to keep up and if you do it successfully, you must find time to discuss what children have written in order to value it.

Development

I developed this idea into recording class Mindset moments. In the first class with whom I worked on Mindset ideas, the Fixed Mindset behaviour was so prominent that I wanted them to see how much damaging behaviour they were exhibiting without realising. I wanted to make it visible. I created a chart that had two sides to it. One side was for Fixed Mindset Moments (in red) the other side was for Growth Mindset moments (in green). I prepared some green and red stars cut out of card and every time one of the children had either of these moments it was written on the back of the star and stuck on the chart. The aim was to visibly reduce the number of red stars that were being stuck on and increase the number of green. It worked and really got the kids on board and working as a team.

In another class, one of the children volunteered to write down any class moments where a mistake was made that we then learnt from together. I found a cuddly 'Brain Cell' www.giantmicrobes.com which I purchased. At the end of the week, we considered the mistakes made over the week and voted on the best one we had learnt from. The person who had made it then got to take the brain cell home that weekend!

Further development

I have now developed this idea further and have made a class **'Mindset Twitter™'** board. Each of the children in the class has a laminated strip of paper, with their name on. They can record their 'Growth Mindset Moments' over the week, at the end of the week, we look at them together. I will pick three of the best (in my opinion) and the children then vote on the Mindset moment of the week. The child who made it will then get to take the Brain Cell home for the weekend. With more and more technology available to schools such as ipads and class homepage, this could be a platform to use with these ideas.

Mindsets at home

With the Brain Cell award, the child also takes home a specially decorated notebook. This notebook has the Mindset labels stuck into the cover and a note to ask families to discuss 'Mindset' at home with their child. They are asked to come up with a family **'Mindset Moment'** that has occurred over the weekend. **This helps to get the messages talked about and understood at home.** It also reinforces the child's understanding as they must explain it to their families. This is a great way of getting families on board. One of the more difficult aspects around creating the culture in school is that children go home at the end of the day. If the Mindset messages are being contradicted at home, this can damage the steps made in school. By educating the families, everybody benefits. Indeed, I have had logs made in the journal about how brothers and sisters have shown Fixed Mindset and the child has explained this to them and helped them to become more Growth in their Mindset!

The logs made in this book are a fantastic piece of evidence to read that shows how children are thinking about their Mindset. It makes good reading for parents when the book is taken home. This activity has proved to be very powerful and something the children have really been motivated by. I love it when a child says, "I could use that as my Tweet this week!" Every week, I am amazed by the quality of the moments they choose to record. Over time, the children who are weaker at finding their 'Tweet' are trained by others around them when they hear the kinds of moments others are writing about.

I was so delighted in finding the cuddly Brain Cell that I purchased one for every class in the school to use in a similar way! The children have come up with various names including Nom Nom the Neuron and Brian the Brain Cell!

Motivational quotes

There are many great quotes that relate really well to the ideas of the Growth Mindset. The website 'Pinterest' is a particularly good place to find some of these quotes that have been made into posters and can be printed. I have compiled a 'Growth Mindset' Pinterest board that is linked through my website **www.growthmindset.org** where such quotes and images can be found.

I have found that children respond to these quotes and process what they mean with interest. Indeed, I have seen and heard children repeating them in different contexts. I have displayed many around school and in my classroom and I have observed children from afar as they go to read them and consider what they mean. Children have come to me to tell me their favourites; it is delightful. I had one child in my class who repeatedly told me that their favourite quote was:

'If Plan A didn't work, the alphabet has 25 more letters! Stay cool.'

The quotes can be very powerful and are a good reference point.

Mindset Celebrities

Quotes can also come from well known people who have achieved highly but have experienced struggle and challenge in order to get where they are. I have a **'Mindset Committee'** who meet together in order to find quotes and pictures of these types of people. We have a **'Celebrity of the Month'** Growth Mindset display in the foyer of the school and the committee compile together material to go up on this board. Example celebrities have included; J.K Rowling, Will Smith, Andy Murray, Albert Einstein, Michael Jordon... The list goes on. There is ALWAYS something in the news that echoes the messages. I am always hearing comments by people being interviewed where I think, 'I can use that!' You just have to keep your ears open and get the children to be on the look-out too: **'Growth Mindset Spotters!'**

A teacher in school came to me recently with a newspaper clipping with the following quote from an article: **'You're not a failure because you didn't succeed; you're a success because you tried.'** Another colleague started to spot motivational postcards in shops that she bought to put up in her downstairs toilet! She started to write them down for me. Everybody should be on a 'Growth Mindset quote' mission!

One of the children in my class made me a card at the end of the year with Growth Mindset pictures and quotes on the front. One of the best cards I have received from a student!

A Gallery of Growth Mindset Quotes

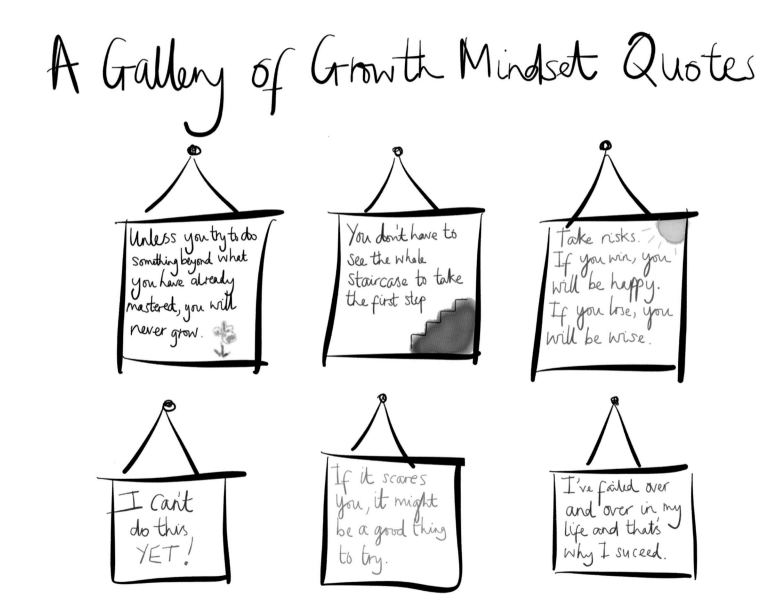

Unless you try to do something beyond what you have already mastered, you will never grow.

You don't have to see the whole staircase to take the first step

Take risks. If you win, you will be happy. If you lose, you will be wise.

I can't do this, YET!

If it scares you, it might be a good thing to try.

I've failed over and over in my life and that's why I suceed.

Target board and fried egg

One of the earliest creations to come out of Mindset theory in the classroom was the creation of a 'Learning Target Board.'

This was the first tool used in all Key Stage 2 classrooms that started to show me how important language is in creating a school Mindset culture. Because we all had it in our classrooms, it instilled a common learning language across the key stage. You could go into another classroom and talk in relation to the learning target board and all the children would know what you were talking about.

What's the big idea?

The Bulls Eye - This represents a person's comfort zone. It is the 'stuff' you know and are comfortable with. Many children want to continue to produce work that comes from this level as it is 'easy' and reassuring for them because they know it.

The Middle Ring - This represents a person's '**Learning Zone**'. This is the layer we start to explore when we start to leave our comfort zone. It is where we start to feel a bit 'shaky' and unsure because it is 'stuff' we don't know so well that we need to practise in order to feel secure. This is where children who don't 'get it' right away may well give up as they don't like the feelings they experience when they are in this place. They don't understand that we all experience these feelings at certain times when learning different things. They don't understand that in order to learn and get better, this zone needs further exploration in order for consolidation to occur.

The Outer Ring - This represents the '**Frustration Zone**'. This was the first name given to this zone but it was felt that this was a little negative and therefore it was re-Christened '**The Break-Through Zone**'. This is where the really difficult challenges are located. It may be that children need to take a step back into the '**Learning Zone**' if tasks in this zone prove too difficult at first. They may not be there **YET** but it is certainly somewhere they could get to if they put in the effort and practise needed to get there.

This visual representation of learning is about showing children that learning is never static. It is always moving and changing. What at first is part of the '**Learning Zone**' will, with enough effort and practise, eventually sit in the Comfort zone. What at first may be in the

'**Break Through Zone**' for children should start to move into the '**Learning Zone**' as they become more confident in tasks that will help them to get there and '**Break Through**'.

Turning the target board on its head

As an aside, I have had the discussion that the middle part of a target board is the Bull's Eye and usually where one is aiming. However, you will see that the model on the next page develops from this idea which would not work if the comfort zone was on the outside. I would also suggest that the target here relates more closely to Vygotsky's 'Zone of Proximal Development' model where the central zone is what the learner can do unaided and the outside zone is what the learner cannot do.

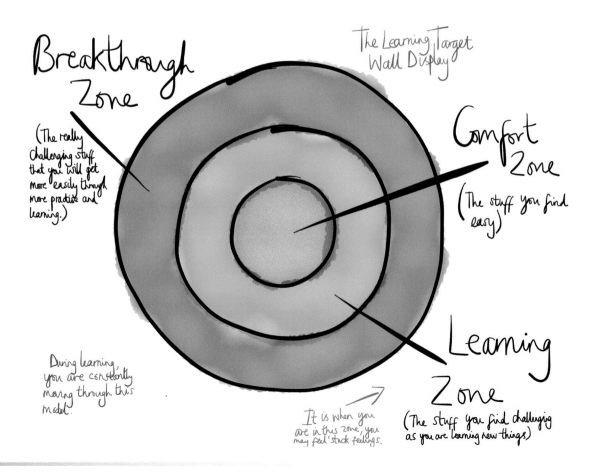

Breakthrough Zone

(The really challenging stuff that you will get more easily through more practise and learning.)

The Learning Target Wall Display

Comfort Zone

(The stuff you find easy)

Learning Zone

(The stuff you find challenging as you are learning new things)

During learning, you are constantly moving through this model.

It is when you are in this zone, you may feel 'stuck' feelings.

Learning is about the journey, not just the destination

I loved working with this idea with children. It illustrates that **learning is a continual process, a journey; it is not static.** One day, your biggest challenges will move and sit in your comfort zone if you put in effort and perseverance to move them. The metaphor also **gives children a language** to express themselves and how they feel in regards to their learning.

I remember once teaching a maths lesson and at the end, a girl came to me with tears of frustration in her eyes. She told me that she just couldn't do it. I didn't need to say anything in order to reassure her. As it happened, I was standing right next to the target board when she approached me. All I did in response to her obvious upset and frustration was point at the 'Breakthrough (Frustration) Zone' and then the 'Learning Zone'. She looked at where I was pointing, thought about what it meant for a moment, looked back at me and smiled. There was understanding between the two of us. She realised and understood at that moment that what she was feeling was normal. It wasn't that she couldn't do it and that was that. She just couldn't do it YET. She also knew that in order to get there, she needed to practise what we had been learning. Instead of stopping and giving up, she knew what she had to do to get there. All of that knowledge and communication gained in one point at a display! Think what that could do for children with English as an Additional Language (EAL) as well.

Fried egg metaphor

A fun metaphor to develop the target board is the notion of using a fried egg to illustrate the same process in learning. The idea is this;

- **The Yolk of the egg** = the 'Comfort Zone' (the yummy yolk!)

- **The Egg White** = the 'Learning Zone' (the white is wobbly and unset whilst in the cooking process before it firms up, just like when you're learning – one of my Year 6's came up with this idea whilst it was being introduced to them.)

- **The Frazzled Crispy Edge** = the 'Break Through Zone' (indeed many of the teachers would often be heard saying they were at their 'Frazzled Crispy Edge' in the staffroom!)

When this was introduced to Year 6, the teacher I was working alongside and myself began the session by playing a clip from the internet of a fried egg being cooked in a pan (we did not want to assume that all the children had witnessed this!) It actually caused a bit of a buzz as we said nothing, just played the clip. They were giggling, wondering why they were being shown this! The more astute children made the connection between this and the display that had suddenly appeared in the classroom! The following discussion about how it related to learning was delightful and a new language was thus introduced. There is now a beautiful material, padded egg in the school foyer which greets you when you enter the school!

Can you create your own metaphors?

When issued with a creative challenge to explore the messages of Mindset in their own way, there were some children in my class who created their own versions of this metaphor and made models to go with them! (I'm still not sure about the stone of a plum as representative of the comfort zone!).

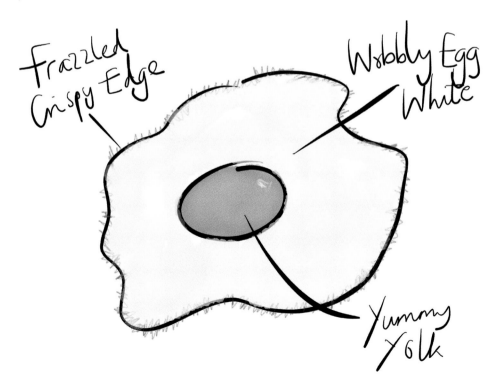

Frazzled Crispy Edge

Wobbly Egg White

Yummy Yolk

Stuck moments

One of the important lessons for children to learn coming from Mindset is the idea that when we get stuck on a task, we feel certain emotions that do not feel particularly good. The problem many children have is they are flooded with negative emotions at times when they start to struggle, particularly if other individuals around them may not be struggling quite as much with that particular task. Children need to understand two things;

1. We all struggle at different things as everybody is different.
2. When we experience struggle, we all feel negative emotions.

Part of the power of knowing about Mindset is that it gives us the awareness to try to switch off these negative feelings (or at least dull them) and embrace what is left. We should all try to treat these feelings more positively and use them to motivate us rather than turn us off and allow them to let us give up on a challenge.

How do you feel when you 'can't do this'?

A useful Mindset activity is the discussion about how we feel when we are stuck and reflecting on some of these moments experienced. The children could then be photographed pulling faces that illustrate these emotions. The pictures could then be printed and displayed in the classroom as a constant reminder not to let these emotions get the better of us in our times of struggle. Another useful reference point for this idea is to think about what happened to Fortitude in my picture book, 'I Can't Do This'.

How do you feel when you have 'done it'?

You could follow up this discussion about how you feel when you accomplish something that you have found challenging. These emotions could be displayed in the same way. It should be reflected that these feelings would not be so great if we had found the task easy. Often the best achievements are the ones we have worked hardest to gain. These are also the things we will remember in the future.

How does 'achievement' when you have worked hard for something feel? – (Find examples of things the children have done).

How does 'achievement' when you have not tried very hard make you feel? – (When you have stayed in your comfort zone and found the task easy).

In KS1 or KS2, try using the feeling faces idea with a visual of 'The Pit' as discussed by James Nottingham. When the children find learning challenging and they feel stuck, they are in the pit. Pictures of the children pulling faces of how they feel at this time could sit inside an image of the pit and faces of how they feel when they have achieved a challenging task on the top when they have managed to climb out of the pit.

anxious   frustrated   Sad   Confused

How does stuck make you feel?

Brain books

Practise, Practise, Practise

A colleague of mine, taking on Growth Mindset principles with her Year 3 class gave them all brain books / folders. At the beginning of the year, each of the children were asked to think of something they thought they needed to practise in order to get better at it. These were SMART goals (i.e., specific short tasks that were achievable in a short space of time) such as particular times tables, handwriting, spellings, etc.

Every day, for ten minutes after lunch, the children would practise the task they had chosen. The children were encouraged to consider when they felt they were ready to move onto the next goal. The fact that they had chosen what they were practising was another way in which the children were encouraged to be more independent about their own learning. The children were encouraged to think about what they needed to practise and agree it with the teacher.

When these children felt they were ready for the next challenge to practise, they would talk to the teacher to check that she agreed and they would agree the next challenge together. At the end of the year, she expressed how well this had worked and that children were making quicker progress in these small steps in the learning than she had witnessed in other Year 3 classes she had taken.

The Growth Mindset Learning Curve

Struggle and stuck.

YET!

(this is the learning danger-zone where you could give up but where your growth mindset needs to kick in.)

I can't do this...

PRACTICE
EFFORT
PERSEVERANCE
MISTAKES

Flick that Mindset switch
(Use your learning buttons)

G.M ON

growing

Score!

seed

flower

Projects

Drama and roleplay

What is the brain and why is it important?

Activities

Mindset Worlds

Writing Opportunities

Assemblies

Galleries

Group Mindset Labels

Projects

Let children explore the messages creatively

One of the best bits about teaching Mindset has been seeing how children choose to creatively explore the messages themselves. Once the children have been working with the principles of Mindset for a little while, a really good way of seeing how they understand them is to set them a **Mindset Project** to explore the messages in any way they choose. Give them the task of conveying the ideas somehow to someone who doesn't know anything about Mindset. What are the main messages and why are they important?

Parental involvement

I have taken some photographs of some of the different offerings I have seen which can be found on my website www.growthmindset.org. If set as a long term homework project, it is also a good way of **getting the parents involved**. Many children have been great at reiterating the messages of Mindset at home, which is very powerful, and explaining them to their parents to encourage them to show Growth Mindset behaviour! In putting together their own projects to explore Mindset, children can be very creative and it is interesting to see how they explore the messages in different ways.

Some ideas have included:

- A shoebox classroom using Lego figures with speech bubbles coming from their mouths with Fixed or Growth Mindset comments – the classroom was halved so that one half contained figures saying Fixed Mindset statements and the other half saying Growth Mindset statements. There were even small posters on the wall depicting these kind of messages.

- A board game with cards to be picked up when the player landed on particular spaces on the board. The cards suggested the player made a Growth or Fixed Mindset comment and therefore should move forward or backward a certain number of spaces accordingly.

- A wooden spoon with a face attached to the head made out of card. One side was smiling whilst the other was sad, the attributes of the Fixed and Growth Mindset were attached to the relevant side of the spoon.

- A model of the brain made out of big polystyrene pieces stuck to thick card and then connected by pictures of neurons firing.

- A collage of Growth and Fixed Mindset quotes (on either half of a piece of A3 paper) – there was even a small 3D box attached with the words, 'Think outside the box' written next to it!

- A tablet box for 'Growth Mindset' tablets – the packet explained what it would help to cure (Fixed Mindset) and possible side effects (i.e. you achieve more but it might give you a headache as you work hard!)

- A set of steps cut out of cardboard, each step displaying statements going from 'I can't do this' progressing gradually from Fixed to Growth Mindset statements. The top step read 'I've done it!'

Photographs of these projects can be found at **www.growthmindset.org**.

Give children the messages and then let them explore them – the results can really make you smile!

Drama and role-play

My original degree was in Psychology and Drama – the psychology interest and background may go some way to explaining my interest in the Mindset Theory and the Drama element is a particularly useful means by which to explore it.

Drama games

I have adapted and used some drama games from my past to begin exploring the different labels of both the Fixed and the Growth Mindset in order to start remembering what defines them.

Role-play is a great way to explore these ideas once they are at the point of being recalled. The idea is that you want children to not only recall what the labels are but then start to link them to behaviours that they then recognise in themselves and others. It is at this point that they can decide if they want to show a certain type of behaviour and ultimately what this will mean in terms of their learning.

Empowering Children

I have known very few children who, after having worked with the Mindset principles, have decided that having a Fixed Mindset towards learning new things is a good idea. If they have veered towards this behaviour, it is usually because other, dominant forces, are at play and these are different issues that the majority of children are not effected by. The power of Mindset is that it allows children to decide what they want from learning – **do they want it to help them to achieve more by exploring, practising and putting in effort or do they want to achieve less by doing none of the latter?**

Applying the Mindset ideas to real life scenarios

I have used role-play in order to explore learning situations with children. It helps to explicitly show how learning situations could be played out differently depending on whether Fixed or Growth Mindset attitudes are adopted. With older children (Year 5 and 6, age 9-11) I have often left the situation that they play out to them (I have found they enjoy the freedom of being able to choose it for themselves). For younger children, you could give them some different learning scenarios where a challenge is encountered; having a particular set of maths challenges offered to them in class (maybe related to what you are learning at the time); having an artistic task given to them and finding it tricky; reading out something in front of an audience for assembly and being nervous; learning to play a tune on an instrument that won't go right. For whatever learning scenario they/you choose, it offers a challenge to the group/individual in the role-play. Ask the children to play out the situation in a Fixed Mindset way, for example:

- They could get stuck and give up and have learnt nothing.

- They could say to themselves that they don't want to look silly in front of everyone so they will pick the easiest option to ensure they achieve it perfectly, again resulting in learning nothing new.

- They are pleased when they get everything right even though it was easy for them, again learning nothing new.

- When others do well, they don't like it.

- They are threatened by others' success rather than learning something new from them and being inspired.

Give these ideas to children to start them off and ask them if they can think of other ways people might show a Fixed Mindset through their behaviour.

However the role-play is played out, the children must refer to the Fixed Mindset labels they learnt to suggest to them how the role-play could end.

Starting point to explore

The children are encouraged to apply the Mindset labels they have learnt previously to real life situations they might well find themselves in. The resulting discussion from watching these performances is therefore a crucial part of this exercise as you explore together what has been played out. The group then need to perform the same situation but this time with the Growth Mindset outcome. The order of whether the situation is played out Fixed followed by Growth could alter; it does not really matter. What does matter is the comparison and the discussion of this. **What the children should see is how a learning situation could be played out so differently, all dependent on which Mindset they choose to adopt in the face of challenge.**

Another way in which to get children to explore what Growth and Fixed Mindset means is to get them to draw/paint their own Mindset worlds. What would be happening in each? What would each look like? Children can be a lot more creative than adults and their ideas could well take you in new directions for discussion. The children should be able to explain their creations and therefore, this is another activity that would allow them to process what Fixed and Growth Mindsets are.

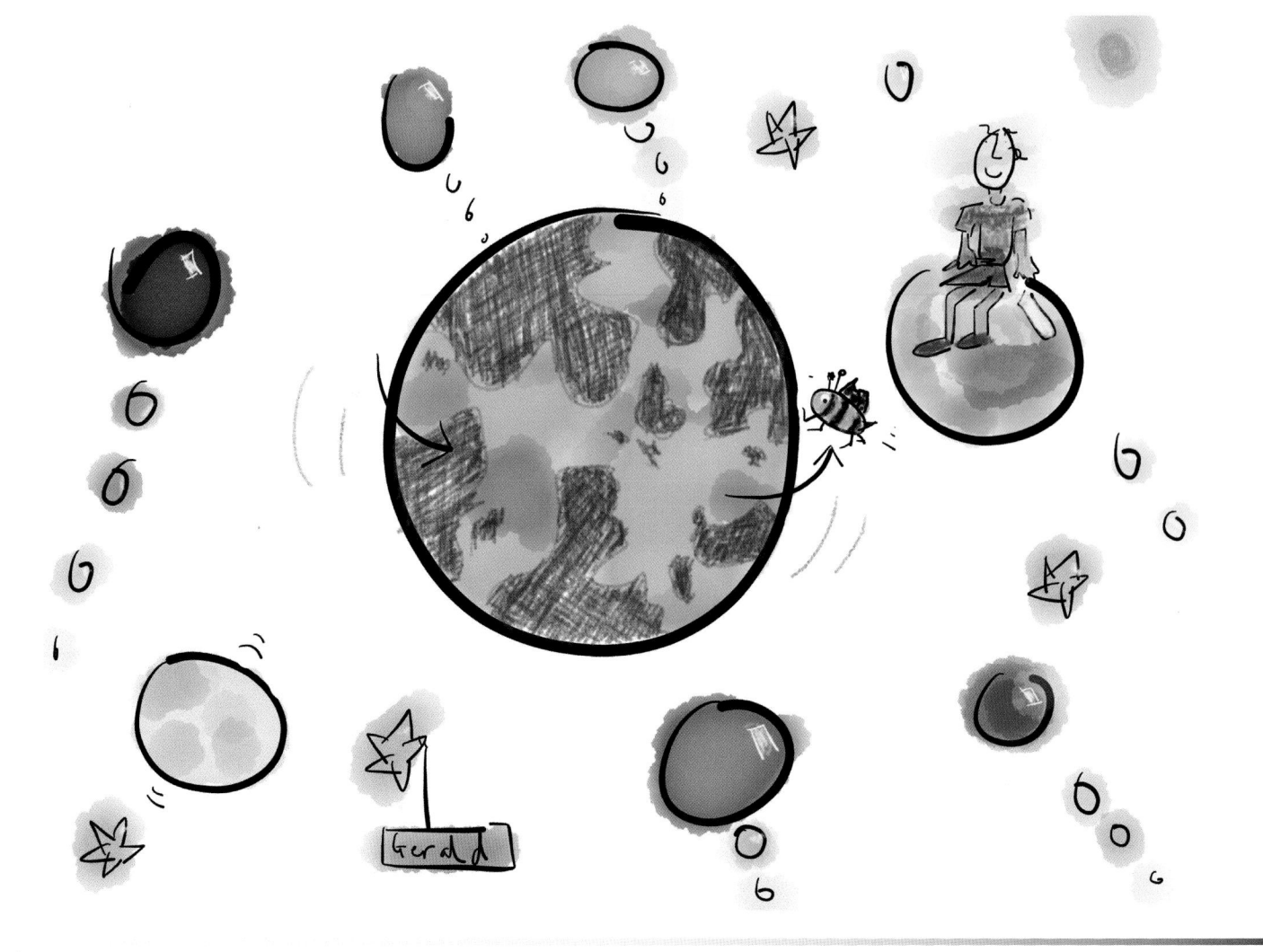

What is the brain and why is it important?

Mindset seeds

As the Flower diagrams (explored in '**Beginnings**', page 37/38) clearly show, the seeds from which the Fixed and the Growth Mindset germinate are different but are both concerned with the brain. It is these different ideas about how the brain works that lead to the behaviours that make up the different Mindsets.

The Fixed Mindset believes that we are born with a certain amount of intelligence and that this does not change. The brain is considered to be a fixed entity and therefore intelligence cannot develop.

Conversely, the Growth Mindset believes that the brain is not a fixed entity and we can develop our intelligence. Through practise and effort, our brain fires new connections between neurons and it is these paths being strengthened that lead to us being able to learn new things. We can 'grow' and develop our intelligence.

Learn about the brain

In school, a 'Brain Afternoon' was held to allow all the children to think about the importance of their brains. A local Neuroscientist from a pharmaceutical company came into a school assembly to talk to the children about Neurons and why they are special. The book, 'My Fantastic Elastic Brain' by Joann Deak (available on Amazon) was read to them with the pictures shown through the Smart Board. This introduced the children to the different parts of the brain; what they do and what they are called.

For KS2 children, an analogy of building muscle using weights was made to building neurons in the brain. A set of weights were lifted by a volunteer in the assembly. A second, heavier pair were then given to be lifted – a more difficult challenge. The link was made that the more a weight lifter practised lifting the heavier weights, the easier it would become as more muscle would be developed. In the same way, the more a challenging activity was practised, the stronger the pathway made by the firing of neurons would become and therefore the easier the task would become. Going back to the analogy of the egg, the challenge would move closer to the Yummy Yolk (or the **comfort zone**).

Brain activities

The children then went back to the classroom and made Brain Hats which can be found on **www.ellenjmchenry.com** along with a song about the brain which can be downloaded. It was all good fun and was actually some great science learning too!

There are also some video clips I have found particularly useful and interesting to children about learning and the brain:

- 'The Learning Brain' available on YouTube. This is now also available as a BBC Learning Zone clip.

- 'How we Learn– Synapses & Neural Pathways' also available on YouTube.

Brain project

The school in which I am currently teaching gives children challenges each term where they are given an open homework task to complete on a particular theme. They then share their projects with other children in the school by way of a 'walk round'. The theme of the last project was 'The Brain' so the children did their own research about and creative expression of the brain.

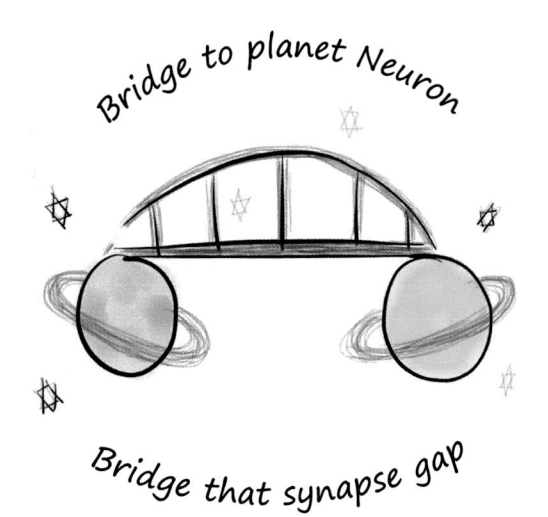

Bridge to planet Neuron

Bridge that synapse gap

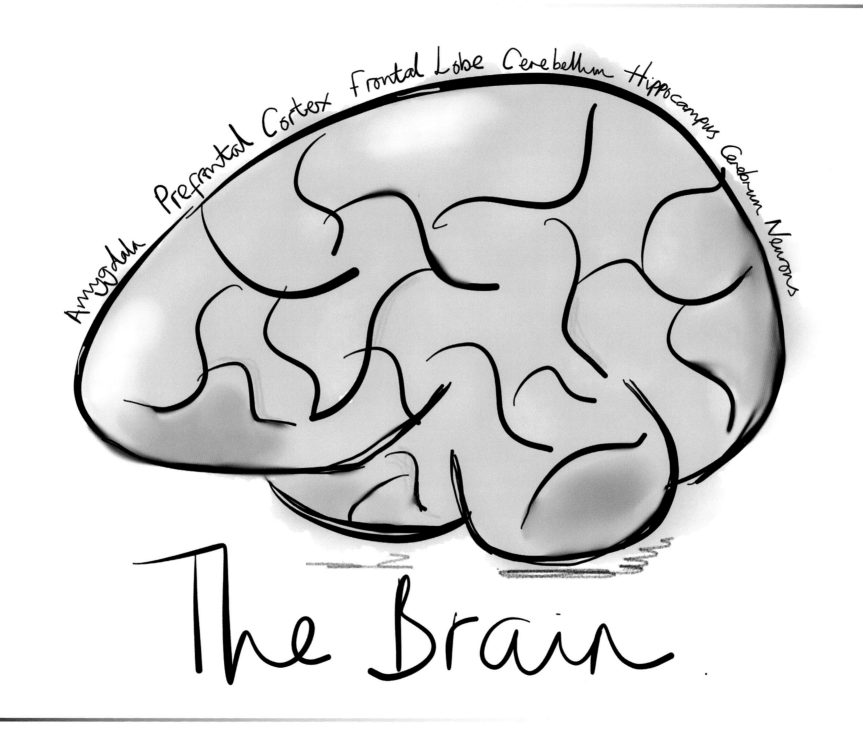

Assemblies

The very first assembly I led about Mindset began with all of the lights switched off in the assembly hall. I began by asking the children if there was anybody who could make light for me as I could not see any of them. I needed light and I needed one of them to make light for me. There was a little giggling and slowly, one by one, children started to put up their hands. I chose one girl and asked her, "Do you think you can really do it? Can you make light happen?" She giggled and nodded. She then walked over to the hall light switches and flicked all of them to the 'on' position. I gasped and said, "Wow! I wanted to make light, you decided you could do it and **YOU** made it happen! Just because you made a decision in your head, you set out to do something and you did it! Well done, let's give her a big round of applause everyone!" Which is what they all did with some smiles and giggles.

I then switched tack completely and the rest of assembly was based around talking about Mindset and showing them the different labels that were printed and laminated onto cards. I asked for volunteers to come to collect a card from a pile that were muddled up and had both Mindset ideas presented on them. Their job was to go and pin them up on the wall with the correct label – either Fixed or Growth Mindset.

I encouraged discussion about certain points and asked them if they could think of any examples in their life that illustrated some of the labels. At the end of the assembly, I referred back to the light scenario at the beginning. I asked if any of the children understood why I had begun the assembly in such a way. The answer is that it shows how **your Mind ultimately controls what you decide to do**. The girl at the start of the assembly had decided that she wanted to make light for me and therefore she was able to do it. **My point was that we all have the power over our brains and therefore we are the only ones who can ultimately decide if we are going to take a Fixed or Growth Mindset approach to life and learning**. If we want to achieve something, nobody else can have that underlying control that drives you to do it. Only you. If you want to achieve, then the Growth Mindset is the one that will get you there. If you decide this is the right path for you, think about the way you behave in relation to your learning.

A regular assembly on Growth and Fixed Mindset ideas is certainly a good way to keep a school reminded of the values together.

The birth of 'Learning Buttons'

It was from this assembly (see previous page) that '**Learning Buttons**' was born. I thought about the idea of control as this is at the foundation of Mindset. First of all you need to know what the Mindsets are in order to be aware of the behaviours that lead to both. It is the **umbrella** to learning as it sits over all the **strategies of learning** that you then put into play. Without the Growth Mindset in place, the strategies are worthless. This is part of your '**Control Button**'. The reason it became a button was because it is like you have to flick a switch in your brain. Pressing buttons is a way of controlling something and making something happen. That is what you must do metaphorically in you mind – press your '**Control Button**' to control having the Growth Mindset. This will then **allow** the other strategies (Buttons) to be pressed.

Connecting Learning Together

I then developed the idea of switch type buttons to buttons used to connect fabric – however, in this sense we are connecting bits of learning together rather than fabric! The analogy of buttons also allows for a lot of interpretation in terms of display and 'button jars' that could be filled up by a class as a reward system when different 'Learning Buttons' are pressed in the class. I have found children like the imagery and tangible, collectable nature of buttons. This is something to play with.

Galleries

Starting Point: Viewing wander

I have observed some amazing discussions between children in relation to learning by setting up **'Silent Galleries'** after some work has been completed. The idea is that children leave their work on their table and then wander around the classroom to observe the different offerings from all of the pupils in the group. The children are then asked to stand behind one piece of work that they particularly like for some reason. Throughout this process, they do not speak. It is a 'silent gallery'!

Development: Why did you choose that one?

The children are then randomly asked why they have chosen to stand behind a particular piece of learning. The children are guided by considering the success criteria given but often they will suggest other reasons as to why they like it, for example they may talk about a particular 'Learning Button' the pupil has obviously used which the work has benefited from. The children could also be asked to look at the work in terms of the effort they think that has gone into it, how do they know? **What are the visible signs of effort?**

Impact

Whenever I have carried out this exercise, the children never just stand behind one piece of work and it has never been the same children chosen whenever I have run it. It is an exercise that is very effective in:

- Getting children to 'up their game' in terms of what they produce (you need to tell them that you are going to do it at the start of the lesson so that they know it is coming and they are ready for it)

- **Boosting confidence** as children have their work selected by their peers

- **Guiding their thinking about learning as they discuss why they like it**

- Exposing the listening children to 'learning' conversation, which, with more exposure helps them to replicate it more independently.

Being inspired by others' success

This exercise supports the aspect of Growth Mindset which reflects **being inspired by other people's success rather than be threatened by it.** It is very important for children to consider why a piece of learning is successful and equally why it is not so successful. They can compare, judge and express for themselves what produces good learning outcomes and will be more inspired to work hard and replicate it themselves. After all, that is what teachers see when they are marking a set of work from a class. Why not let children go through the same process and make these comparisons themselves? That is powerful. Ask the children about work they have selected:

> **'Why is this piece of learning good?'**
> **'How do you know they have put in effort?'**
> **'What would make this even better?'**

The satisfaction experienced from being praised for effort and unpicking the strategies used to get there is a much greater reward than just, 'this is a great piece of work,' a sentiment that is short-lived. In being **specific** about what is good, the learner will gain much more information that they can replicate and build on in the future. In having the discussion, children receiving the information, the child giving the information and those around them listening to the discussion are shown HOW to produce good learning and are hearing quality talk about learning that is being generated by their peers. **Everybody wins!**

Writing opportunities

Get creative!

There are some great writing opportunities that could come from children learning about Mindset. In thinking about literacy genres, independent writing and Talk for Writing (Pie Corbett), here are some creative opportunities that could be explored:

- How to catch a Fixed Mindset (instructional writing).

- How to catch a Growth Mindset (instructional writing).

- A letter to the Head / another school about why they should learn about Mindset (persuasive writing).

- Why a Growth Mindset is better than a Fixed Mindset (debate followed by a Persuasive argument text).

- What are Mindsets? (Explanation text).

- Recounting a day when Mindset behaviour has taken place (recount/diary entry).

- An information leaflet about what the different Mindsets are (information text).

- Mindset inspired poetry using techniques they have learnt/are learning about.

- A narrative about an individual with a Fixed or Growth Mindset (what was the problem that was encountered and how was it resolved?).

- A narrative set in a Growth/Fixed Mindset world (this could be written after a piece of art work exploring the same idea has been created as a starting point).

- Growth Mindset Haiku and Kenning poetry. These are great for processing the Fixed and Growth Mindset attributes. **This would be a great first activity to do when starting to process the messages and embed them.** A colleague and I challenged each other to write a Fixed and Growth Mindset Kenning. What we came up with is detailed on the following page:

Growth

Mind chooser, constant trier, risk taker, comfort-zone buster, feedback listener, mistake maker, person inspirer, go getter, ideas seeker, resource user, understanding mover, life progresser, challenge doer, brain expander, neuron firer, improvement maker, de-bugger, opportunity opener, challenge confronter, learning stretcher, risk taker, setback coper, task perseverer, world explorer, from mistakes learner, talent developer, eye opener, ideas connector, can't yetter, feedback user, friendly critiquer, world changer, intelligence developer, effort maker, big achiever, forever learner.

Fixed

Challenge avoider, feedback hater, giver upper, mistake hider, criticism loather, effort skirter, get it all righter, tick lover, intelligence protector, brain stays the samer, non-risker, effort shirker, opportunity rejector, can't do it-er, achieve lesser, intelligence stopper, praise depender, thought interferer, intelligence harmer, ability blocker, mind barrier, door closer,

Here are some Haiku poems that Year 4 children created following the syllable pattern 5,7,5 for the lines:

Growth Mindset is good (5)
Be inspired by others (7)
See what you can do! (5)

I can't do this yet (5)
I kept trying at my maths (7)
I can do it now! (5)

I am sure this is the tip of the literacy iceberg but hopefully these ideas will inspire your own creative exploration.

Behaviours

- 'I don't know!' moments
- Marking and Feedback
- Clearing Strategies: cleaning Buttons
- Applauding Mistakes
- Language
- Rewarding Growth Mindset behaviours

Rewarding Growth Mindset behaviours

There is a section in Dweck's 'Mindset' book in which she talks about a young girl who has already decided where she'll put the rosettes she's expecting to win at a forthcoming gymnastic competition. When she is not placed, she is devastated. The reader is asked to consider what the parents should say to her;

1. Tell the girl you thought she was the best.
2. Tell her she was robbed of the ribbon that was rightfully hers.
3. Reassure her that gymnastics is not that important.
4. Tell her she has the ability and will surely win next time.
5. Tell her she didn't deserve to win.

Praise

Dweck goes on to discuss the underlying message given to children by each response. It is the fifth option that is the right Growth Mindset option but it is not fed back to the child in quite that way which is somewhat harsh! The point is that you want children to consider that if they really want to achieve something, they must work for it.

The parents of Elizabeth told her that if she really wanted to win next time, she should put in more practise in order to improve. They said that the girls that did win ribbons probably had put in more hours and therefore deserved the ribbons they won. (I have actually discussed this scenario and the options the parents had with some year 6 children which made for an interesting discussion). The reason for referring to the scenario above is that, as teachers, parents and role models, we must be careful about for what we give praise and what we say specifically in our praise. There are two different types of praise which give very different underlying messages to children;

Intelligence praise

This is where (in the context of the classroom or home) children are praised for excellent pieces of work / scores because they must be really smart / intelligent / good at it;

"Wow! That's a great picture, you must be really good at art." Or "Great, you solved that maths puzzle really quickly, you are an excellent mathematician!"

This kind of praise makes it more likely that children will stick to the things they know they can do well and do well quickly. Children are less likely to challenge themselves if they are used to getting praised for what they can do well without mistakes. (Going back to the flower diagram of the Fixed Mindset, children have a lot to protect in terms of their intelligence if they believe their intelligence doesn't develop). If we are praising children's intelligence then we are basically feeding the Fixed Mindset. This is a natural thing to do which is why it needs some consideration; *the effects of giving this type of praise can be highly damaging.* **We must be careful that we are not praising intelligence but instead focus on the effort that children have put into learning.**

"Wow! I know how hard you worked on that (if they have). I particularly like how you have graduated the colour so that it goes from light to dark. It makes it very striking."

Process Praise

This is where effort, struggle and perseverance in learning are noted and celebrated with children. If these kind of behaviours are praised and the learning strategies that came with this behaviour are discussed, this will lead children to repeat this kind of behaviour in the future. They will develop these strategies and learning behaviours further as they become part of the culture of the classroom they are working in. It is this behaviour that leads to the best future learning as the right behaviour will be repeated (i.e., taking on new challenges to create new learning). If this culture is developed, children start to pick up on the message from their peers and that has a powerful effect.

This introduction is important in understanding the extraordinarily high value of the reward systems explained in '**Mindset Journal**' and '**Mindset Twitter™**'.

Applauding mistakes

Babies love a challenge!

One of the most important aspects to creating the Growth Mindset culture in the classroom is a whole group understanding and **appreciation of making mistakes**. One of the first things I began to consider when I read Dweck's book was the idea that an individual's Mindset could largely be affected by people around them. Dweck considers how babies go through the biggest challenges that human beings will ever face; learning to walk and learning to talk. They wobble and topple; they fall over and pick themselves up; they babble and squeak and if they are anything like I was as a baby, they copy intonation so that the babble appears to sound like they are actually having a conversation (or so I am told)!

When do we start giving up on challenges?

A baby does not give up in the face of these most difficult of challenges. Dweck asks us to consider exactly when this motivation and drive to work through challenges starts to leave us. Her answer to this? **When we are able to start comparing ourselves and our achievements to other people.** I think she is right and the first time we are all faced with the ultimate opportunity to compare ourselves to others in the face of challenge to learn new things? School.

How it feels to be 'stuck'

I thought about this and the children who sit in every classroom finding it hard to complete a task given to them. Others around them getting on and being able to do the task, possibly with ease. How would you start to feel? Without the bitter experience of 'Growing Up' that we have as adults, I started to really think about how a child, without knowledge to reflect on what was occurring, might start to feel. I related this thought to certain children that I taught and had taught in the past. In the years to come, I will see more and more of these same children, looking around themselves in their **'stuck' moments,** feeling lost and feeling stupid. It is at these moments that children start to shut down and close off from learning.

Misconception revealed leads to feedback and new learning

Thinking back to the flower diagram illustrating the Fixed Mindset monologue, the more these children go through these moments, the more they define themselves by failure. Not a comfortable place to be and if that is what you start to associate with learning and challenges, why WOULD you want any more of them? Especially when other children (possibly Fixed Mindset in a different way) seem to be able to tackle the same challenges with relative ease.

Understanding the value of mistakes

This leads me on to why it is important to harp on in the classroom about **the value of mistakes.** Thinking back to the babies and the challenges they face, they make a multitude of mistakes in order to learn to walk and talk. If they didn't make mistakes, they would not learn how to achieve these challenges. They learn from mistakes how NOT to do things and in so doing, they learn how they SHOULD do things. This idea never changes in relation to challenge. **What does change is our willingness to make those errors in front of others.**

Develop resilience by making it transparent

As a society, we view making mistakes, criticism and negative feedback as bad things. We take these occurrences as a personal attack which hurts us when in actual fact, these are the things that help us to learn. Children need to be taught this explicitly and in understanding this, develop a resilience that will allow them to learn from these happenings rather than be knocked over by them. For some reason, we expect them to know this (as if it is in-built) and, most often, they don't. It is our duty as adults to let them in on this little secret. If all children in the classroom are operating in this way, because what are valued is the mistakes and what is learnt from them, then these children will become more exploratory and willing to take on challenge because it is OK to get things wrong or not 'get it'.

What is more important is what learning comes from the mistake.

In light of all this theory, there is a simple mechanism by which you can start to underpin these values in the classroom and at the end of the day, with all the other aspects of classroom life we must manoeuvre ourselves around as teachers, what we want and need is simple but effective! What you can start to do is this: **APPLAUD MISTAKES.**

Learning from Mistakes

Every time somebody in the class makes a mistake when you are working collaboratively, acknowledge it and make a fuss about it in a positive way! It can and should be done in a fun way that everybody can enjoy! Congratulate the person who made it and together, applaud the mistake. Illustrate that we are all able to learn from the mistake. Discuss the mistake; agree why it is a mistake and then decide together what you have learnt from it. It helps children to remember the tricky aspects to their learning and enables them to overcome these challenges. It informs what they need to remember in order to be successful at the task.

"From failure you learn. From success, not so much."
(Quote taken from 'Meet the Robinson's', Walt Disney Pictures)

You must be mindful about how you introduce this in order not to upset anybody as they start to get used to it. However, I have found the effect to be most powerful and very soon the children start to pick up on your errors as well (yes, we do all make them) and they will enjoy applauding you! At first, this may feel a little odd but it is for exactly the reason that it feels odd that it is effective! It actually reinforces the idea that we all make mistakes, including adults and teachers who, despite appearances, do get things wrong and that getting things wrong is a normal part of life. As long as we learn something from it, making mistakes is OK.

The practice also goes a long way in strengthening trust and relationships in the classroom as everybody, including the adults are allowed to get things wrong. You could even make a **display of the best mistakes made and what was learnt as a result!** The **'Mindset Twitter Wall'** and the award of the Brain Cell will go to strengthen this idea further. The above behaviour could be seen to be 'gimmicky' but gimmicks work with children and they get a lot out of this one!

Marking and feedback

One of the most influential aspects to learning

As I mentioned, there is a lot of information published about how 'Marking & Feedback' can be done effectively so I am not going to write in great detail on this topic. However, a look at the behaviours needed to promote a Growth Mindset attitude in the classroom is not complete without a reference to marking and feedback. It has been shown that this is one of the most influential ways children's learning can be enhanced. From a Growth Mindset perspective, it appears to me that a simple rule of thumb is to ensure that any feedback must:

- Be specific (what is good or needs improvement and why?)
- Reflect the effort that has gone into producing it.
- Allow the children to respond to it.

Be specific

Children need to know what **specifically** is good or needs improvement in their work. Only when armed with this information can they pro-actively attend to it and make the decision as to whether they will work to improve. They must have all the tools/information available in order to make this decision. After all, this is the attitude we are encouraging in embedding the Growth Mindset ideas.

It is important for children to understand **why** praise is being given. It is important that you are **specific** about why you are praising a piece of learning (written or otherwise). If children are to replicate the positive aspect of what they have produced, they need to know what that was. They will want to replicate it in the future because they now know this is the aspect of their learning that you praised because it was good.

Reflect effort

It is useless to simply praise the child for a good piece of work. If any praise is given (written or verbal) it should reflect the effort that the child has put in to producing it, i.e. 'Well done for persevering; I know you found that bit tricky,' instead of, 'Well done, this is an excellent piece of work.' The difference is subtle but the two statements subconsciously give out two very different messages and therefore are likely to bring about two very different behaviours:

1. "Well done, this is an excellent piece of work. You have written a fantastic opening!"

This tells the child that you only value an excellent outcome. It says, 'I will value an outcome that is perfect and has no mistakes.' This is why a child may not venture out of their comfort zone and simply stick to what they know they can achieve with excellence. If they try to do a task that is challenging, something that is out of their comfort zone, they may well make errors and produce something that is not perfect. They know that to get the above sort of praise, they need the outcome to be perfect.

2. "Well done, I can see that you worked really hard on that and that you didn't find it easy. That means you will have learnt new things. You have created suspense by using a number of effective techniques."

With this type of praise being given, the child knows that in order to get approval, they must come out of their comfort zone and try new things that challenge them, therefore they are more likely to exhibit this kind of behaviour in the future. We should be openly celebrating the type of behaviour that this second style of praise is reflecting. It comments on the level of difficulty and perseverance of the task and is also specific about what was done to achieve it that was good. We should be careful to not only praise flawless work that may have involved little effort if the child was not particularly challenging themselves.

I am not suggesting that excellent work should not be rewarded but I think it is important to acknowledge when effort has been significant in both the production of excellent outcomes and ones that may not 'appear' to be excellent but where new challenges have been faced in order for it to have been achieved. Perhaps the excellent outcomes produced by the child in his comfort zone should be met with some discussion about how they could have challenged themselves to explore something new within the work. What 'new' learning could have been occurred?

Allow time for response

The best way to process feedback and understand it to alter future outcomes is to attend to it.

The 'empty praise' police

For older children, the above is a useful and interesting topic for discussion. Which type of praise do they think they should be given? Do they think it is important that the praise they receive should be specific and should appreciate their effort? If so, why? By exploring the idea that praise is an empty mechanism if it does not give them information, they will actually be able to have more meaningful discussions with peers when they praise their learning. They may well start to pick teacher's up on empty praise! This will help to develop this understanding and culture within the teacher's own practise and help them to focus on it. This discussion will lead to 'deep learning' and could have a big impact on the classroom culture.

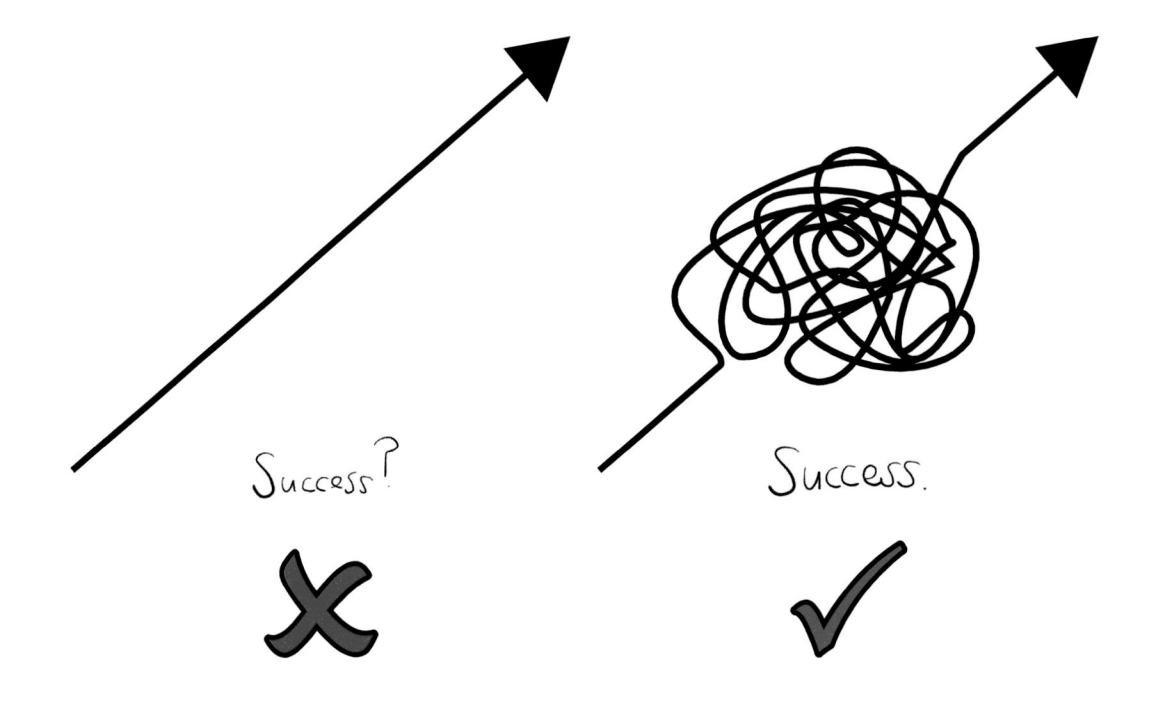

Language

Talking it leads to behaving like it

All the ideas in this book go to creating a **learning language** that everybody in the classroom understands and can talk. It is when this starts to happen that you know you are being successful in creating the Growth Mindset culture. When this occurs, the most powerful learning behaviour will emerge. Once the children can 'talk it' the next phase is to project the messages by behaving in the associated way.

I can't do this

There are particular phrases that support the creation of a 'learning language' that are centred around Growth Mindset principles. One of my favourite phrases was the inspiration for my picture book, '**I Can't Do This**'. The main character, Fortitude (which means to find courage in the face of adversity) has an adventure during which he finds the word **YET** to add to his Fixed Mindset thought, 'I can't do this'. The phrase, '**I can't do this YET**' suggests that you are on a learning curve and that although you may not be able to do something at the moment, with practise and effort you could well achieve your goal in the future.

Not the end of the story

'I can't do this' is not the end of the story which is what I think many young children believe. We need to explicitly teach them this is not the case. This is a phrase that even very young children can be introduced to very successfully. The compilation of a class '**Growth Mindset phrase book**' is another class activity that could be introduced. Quotes could be included in this repertoire. Can the children find their own phrases?! This will all go to helping them talk the talk and own the culture.

'I don't know!' moments

Life and the classroom are full of 'I **don't know**' moments. You need to openly relish and enjoy these moments with the children. Make a big deal about them and openly model to them your own 'I don't know' moments.

Learning is about embracing the struggle

I remember, when I first trained to be a teacher, a lecturer saying that **children think that teachers are like robots that simply store information in their heads.** It is important that children don't think this is the case. If they think that learning is about remembering facts and storing them we are offering a very distorted view of learning that many children would not be interested in. They need to see that teachers are human beings and struggle and are challenged and have to work at new learning, just like them.

Teachers modelling challenge

I had a colleague who told the children she was going to learn to knit. She kept them updated with her progress via a blog. The children delighted in following their teacher's progress in learning a new skill and sharing her highs and lows! (There were quite a few lows!) She shared her mistakes and what she had learnt from them. She also shared her discoveries of herself as a person. A great way for children to appreciate teachers as human beings who learn, just as they do.

Nobody is the finished article; there is always more to learn.
Children need to know that the adults in their life are always learning new things to grow themselves. Everybody should be open about sharing their new discoveries and new learning, however small. They should also be open about HOW they learnt new things- this could be developed into a display that is added to on a regular basis:

HOW WE LEARN NEW THINGS (link these ideas to the 'Learning Buttons' detailed on the following pages).

Learning strategies and buttons

How do we learn?

Once the ideas of Mindset are understood and more widely talked about in relation to learning in the classroom, it is important to develop this conversation into a practical understanding of HOW we learn. **Talking about it is the first step to behaving in a way that emulates the theory.**

Mindset as the umbrella to all learning

If you have developed Mindset so that it is embedded within the everyday running and talk of the classroom, you then need to **use this behaviour as the umbrella to all the other learning strategies that are used in the classroom.** If you make this into a language that everybody uses in the classroom as well, you will create a classroom full of learning talk in which everybody talks the same language and therefore all the high expectations are understood and worked towards by all.

Learning Buttons:

Control, Collect, Connect, Community, Curiosity, Create, Creativity

At the end of my second year working with Growth Mindset, I began to think about the fact that the Mindset part of learning is an umbrella. It is the foundation to all learning. Without the right attitudes in place, children will not be open to any significant learning. They have to be **willing** and that is what the Mindset philosophy is all about. **It is about motivating them to want to learn.** Once this is in place, we need to give children **strategies** to lean on to support them in their learning journeys and give them a way to think and talk about **HOW** they are going to learn.

Through lots of research and from my own experience in the classroom with children, I created 'Learning Buttons'. The idea initially came from an assembly I talked about earlier where I switched off the lights and asked if anyone could create light for me (see 'Assemblies' , page 66 in Activities section of this book). **I had told the children they were the ones in control of deciding if they flicked that Growth Mindset switch in their heads - nobody else.** Having a switch/button gives an individual control over making something happen. **Why not press learning buttons?** Buttons also have the connection to joining fabric to keep it together. **I linked this to the idea of**

learning being about making links and connections to hold ideas/thought together. Buttons are something tangible, something collectable, something good with which to make displays! There are many possibilities in using learning buttons as the metaphor by which to consider learning.

There are certain links to **De Bono's Learning Hats**. I have also read about **Guy Claxton's 4 R's** and **Learning Powers**. I have dipped my toe in the water with all of these educational concepts but somehow, the Learning Buttons came together out of the Growth Mindset completely by chance, it has stuck because it works and children love it! The definitions of each button are a blend of my own ideas from research and from some children that I have worked with. They mind-mapped everything they could think of about how they learnt new things.

Define your own Buttons

If you decide to use the 'Learning Buttons' framework, lead your class through this process too in order for them to define their own Buttons. In thinking about this themselves, the Buttons will mean more to them as they will understand where they came from. Children will generally come up with the same ideas and these should be incorporated into the 7 Buttons in the most appropriate places. All the Buttons begin with the letter 'C' in order to make them easy to remember. In class, the children can use them as another way of talking about their learning, for example **"I think I need to press my creativity button!"** or **"What buttons have we pressed in that bit of learning?"** It gets children thinking about what they are doing when they are learning (a form of Metacognition) and that can help them with future learning. The buttons can also be referred to in rewarding children (e.g. on the Mindset Twitter™ board).

Challenge Button?

Recently, a child suggested that we should add a 'Challenge' button to the list. At first I liked the idea. However, on further consideration, I felt that children should always be challenged and therefore it was not a separate button that we should press for a particular piece of learning. The discussion shows how children engage with the buttons at a deep level in relation to Mindset ideas. **For me, the Buttons are about what strategies we call on at particular moments to help us achieve particular tasks. Challenge should be integral to the task to begin with.**

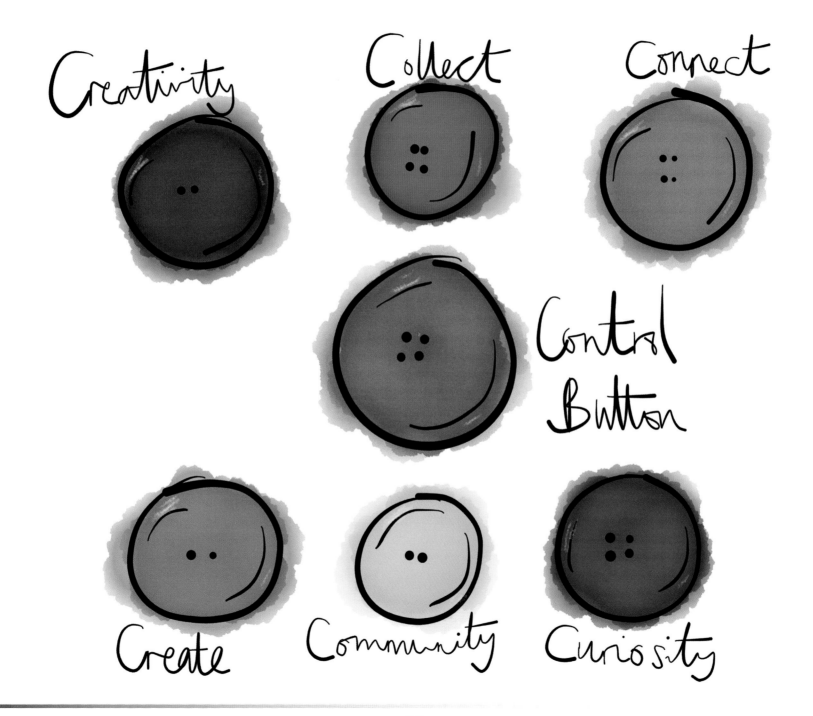

Creativity

Collect

Connect

Control Button

Create

Community

Curiosity

Creativity Button

What if I was made of chocolate?

— Use your imagination
Wonder 'what if...'

— Try thinking about things differently to how they have been thought of before.
Think 'outside the box.'

— Try new things you haven't done before - Explore!

Collect Button

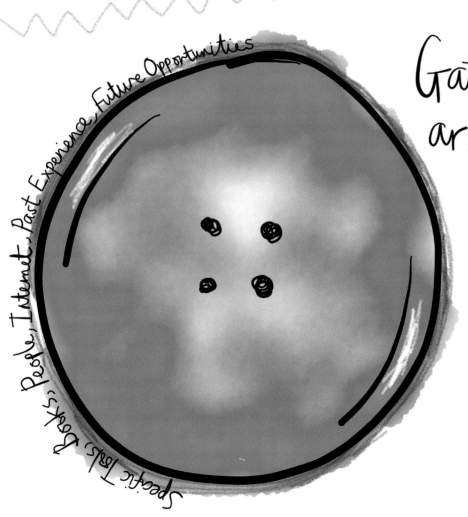

People, Internet, Past Experience, Future Opportunities

Specific Tables, Books,

Gather ideas from all around you (magpie)

What resources do you have around you that might help you?

Connect Button

- Be aware and open to things around you, connect to the world around you.
  - Take opportunities — who knows where it might lead

- Look for connections between events and experiences (that connection may not be obvious to you at first.)

- Spot patterns

- Weave a web of understanding to help you make sense of it — Mindmap!

Control Button

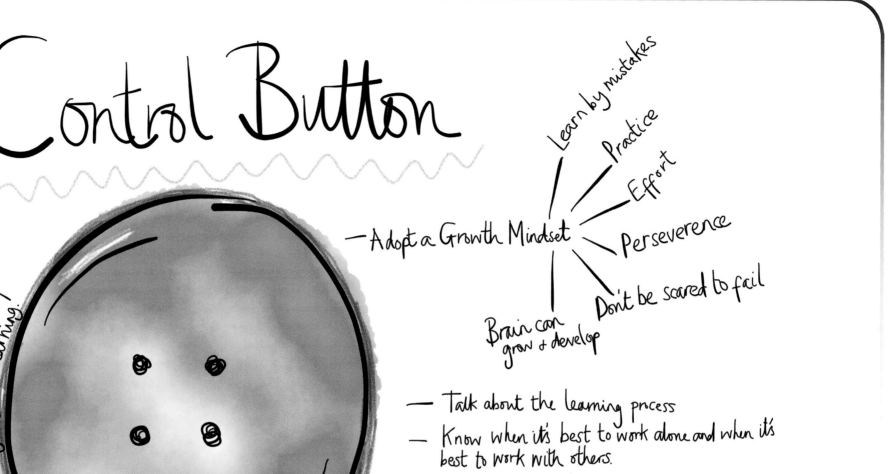

Have fun and enjoy your learning!

— Adopt a Growth Mindset
- Learn by mistakes
- Practice
- Effort
- Perseverence
- Don't be scared to fail
- Brain can grow & develop

— Talk about the learning process
— Know when it's best to work alone and when it's best to work with others.
— Feel the fear and do it anyway.
— Manage distractions
— Understand yourself as a learner — how do you learn best?
— Believe in yourself!
— Know when to press certain learning buttons.
— Be focused and absorbed in your learning.

Create Button

Press all your Learning Buttons!

— Make sure you understand what you need to achieve before you start

— Plan your route before you start

— Change things along the way if you need to. Be flexible.

— Monitor and review your work as you go along.

— Spot new opportunities as they come up.

— Use all skills to produce the best outcome you can.

— Concentrate and focus on the job you are doing.

Question Review Mistakes Method Logical Perseverance Effect Teamwork Curiosity Focus Concentration Patience

Community Button

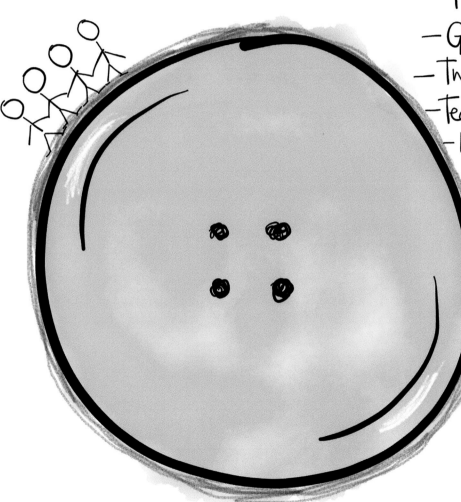

- Magpie ideas
- Give and receive feedback
- Two heads are better than one
- Teamwork
- Listen to others and try to understand what they are saying.
- Adopt useful strategies, habits, values from others you observe.
- Ask questions of yourself and others
- Respect everybody's ideas
- Think about how to combine good ideas together to make something amazing in group work.

Curiosity Button

— Ask questions and try to find out answers.

— Play with ideas — delve beneath the surface of things.

— Notice things around you that might help you.

— Be curious — you never know when you might use something from your experience.

Final word

A multitude of ideas. A 'Melting Pot' if you will. To successfully create a culture from all this there are things that need setting up and that will take the time and the work from you as leader of your classroom. These ideas have come together over a few years and built up to where they are now. No doubt they will be built upon further and I hope to produce a revised edition in the future.

I now hope that others can use this to **begin a new school year** by **putting down these foundations** at the start. The first two or three weeks in the year should be used to set this culture up. The start of the new school year, when you are laying down the expectations of how your classroom will operate, is the perfect time to do this. It forms a large part of your expectations for the year. This is the hardest bit but is worth putting in the time to get it right. You can then refer back to these points regularly throughout the learning day and they will know exactly what you are referring to. **When pupils have 'got it' your life will be easier because children see the point of learning in a way they may not have done before.**

You will start to hear a new kind of learning talk in your classroom that will certainly put a big smile on your face! It will not just be you that talks the learning talk, the children will too and what's more, they'll walk the walk and that will create a classroom of purpose and motivation which is what we all want. Teaching Growth Mindset ideas to children is like **handing them a magic key** that will allow them to unlock the locked door of learning. Many children find this door is stuck fast; they struggle to open it. **If you take the time to set the ideals up in your classroom/school you will certainly reap the benefit of children who want to learn because they understand learning that bit better.**

You need to give children the tools. From then on, the they will run it, develop it, live it and create with it. You will be taken along on their ride and that's what I have enjoyed about building up these ideas. Different groups of children will take it in different directions and you will have ideas that can add to it. This is how the class own it and become independent learners. This is a place from which to start. After all, every journey has to begin somewhere. It is up to us to enjoy the ride and make some good mistakes along the way from which to learn. **We all need to aspire to the values of the Growth Mindset. We all need a little Fortitude.**

Please take a look at the time-line on the following page which suggests how to develop the Growth Mindset culture by considering the order to introduce these ideas to your classroom. To set up the Mindset culture, these activities should be introduced and children guided through them. The other ideas in this book can then be considered around their introduction. Once the ideas are in place, the philosophy can be referred to over the year in a teaching and learning context; the children will know what they mean because you have explicitly taught them the theory.

If you would like to contact me about your thoughts, experiences and questions in adopting these principles, I can be contacted via email through the website **www.growthmindset.org**.

My own picture book, '**I Can't Do This**' explores a key idea of the Growth Mindset. It was written as my first vehicle to open up these ideas with children. The ideas in 'The Mindset Melting Pot' soon followed. I have created guided reading notes to work alongside 'I Can't Do This' with children and these are also available on the website as another means of immersing children in the messages of the Growth Mindset. There are also suggestions as to how to use the text in other subjects.

I can't do this...

Written and illustrated by

K J Walton

Timeline for Mindset Introduction Activities

Have 'What is...' discussions with children

What is intelligence? p39-p42;
What is effort? p43;
What is risk taking? p44;
Why is it OK to make mistakes? p54;
What is the brain and why is it important? p63;
What is it to be 'stuck' and how does it feel? p54-p55

Introduce 'Mindset Twitter'

Put up display with students named 'tweet' cards, set up a Mindset Book to send home and purchase a cuddly brain cell from www.giantmicrobes.com- set up a weekly slot (20 minutes) to talk about children's weekly 'Mindset Tweets' and vote on a winner to take the brain cell home p46

A Vital Starting Point

Labelling body activity p26;
Children group Mindset labels into their own groups p28

'Brilliant! What did we learn from that?'

Applaud mistakes p75-p77

Put up displays

For example, the Egg or Learning Target Board p50-p53;
The Learning Buttons p85-p92;
Stuck Faces p54-p55;
Motivational Quotes p48-p49

Set up and introduce brain books

Practise SMART skills identified by students p56

What are the different Mindsets?

Explore and embed Kim's Game p33;
Indian Teepee p33-p34;
Mindset Football p35;
Drama & Role-play p60-p61;
Flower belief system (where Mindsets stem from) p36-p38

Ideas about 'HOW you learn'

Introduce the 'Learning Buttons' p83-p92;
Integrate their ideas into the buttons;
Refer to Learning Buttons during teaching and learning (explore regularly what buttons they are pressing and why- what has using that button enabled them to do?)

How to keep the ideas sustained over the year

Once the timeline activities have been set up (ideally at the start of the new school year as part of the first few weeks setting up your expectations for the rest of the year), you must integrate these ideas into the day-to-day running of your classroom:

- Have drop-in Mindset Assemblies to keep the messages alive as a school.

- Hold a 'Brain Day'.

- Show children video clips as mentioned at relevant moments.

- Marking and feedback is specific and highlights the effort that has gone in to producing an outcome.

- Praise is specific (what is it the child has done that is good?).

- Avoid praising intelligence and praise effort.

- Find motivational quotes to display (Pinterest is an excellent place to start to this search).

- Celebrity Mindset Spots (set up a 'Celebrity Mindset of the Month' board).

- Set up a 'Mindset Committee' to help keep this board updated.

- Put together a Mindset related story books box - develop ways to use these stories around school. (There is a list of possible texts listed on my Growth Mindset Facebook page which can be reached through the website www.growthmindset.org).

- Relish 'I don't know' moments in class and the explore them to find out.

- Highlight and celebrate adults learning new things.

- Explore the Mindset ideas in subjects (e.g literacy writing for different genres).

- Have regular 'Silent Galleries' for children to look at each other's work to explore what is good and why.

All of the above will go to create a **Growth Mindset language** which everybody in the school should understand and speak.

The Value of the Melting Pot:

$$\frac{\text{Beginnings} + \text{Activities} + \text{Supportive Aids} + \text{Behaviours}}{\text{Growth Mindset Culture}}$$

Your journey is now ready to begin...